JAPAN'S NEW COLONY- AMERICA

Japan's New Colony– America

How We Americans Have Been Brainwashed And Compromised By Japan

What "We the People" Can Do

By **Bernard E. Conor**

Published in the United States by Perkins Press

JAPANS NEW COLONY—AMERICA
HOW WE AMERICANS HAVE BEEN BRAINWASHED AND COMPROMISED BY JAPAN
What "We the People" Can Do

By **Bernard E. Conor**

Copyright © 1991 by Bernard E. Conor

All rights reserved under International and Pan-American Copyright Conventions.
Published in the United States by Perkins Press.

Library of Congress Cataloging-in-Publication Data
Details not available at time of printing.

JAPAN'S NEW COLONY—AMERICA.
ISBN 0-9631145-0-6

Manufactured in the United States of America.

Typography by TeleSet

To:
the Poor, Unemployed, Minorities,
and
other Former Workers
from our
Closed Manufacturing Plants

and

to the Future Graduates
of our High Schools and Colleges
that they may find
a Good Job
in a
Revived American Manufacturing Industry
as we throw off the yoke
of
Japanese Colonialism

Acknowledgments

MANY PEOPLE HAVE given me encouragement and assistance in writing this book. I am grateful for all those people who also have taken their time to keep me informed of so many Japanese actions around the world.

My gratitude to the unknown gentleman at the ASIA conference who pointed out to me that I was probably the only one at the conference who dared ask a hard question—since I was not compromised. This revelation was a major motivation in writing this book.

My **thanks** to Paul Steidlmeier and John Mather for their frank and objective comments in reviewing the book. My appreciation to a major publisher who after reviewing my proposal for the book in early 1990 suggested some excellent changes, in particular the title.

To my wife Mary Lou who has given me so much encouragement and support.

And to all those people who have assisted in so many ways, whose names I cannot mention lest they suffer from Japanese retaliation. □

This book was not written
to make money.
It was written to **Wake Up America.**

**One third of any profits
will be donated to fund a program
to help make America more competitive—globally.**

Why We Need
a New American
Revolution of Independence
by
"We the People."

CONTENTS

FOREWORD iii

INTRODUCTION ix

Section I: **What You Really
　　　　　　Ought To Know About The Japanese** 1

Chapter 1: WHAT JAPANESE ETHICAL
　　　　　　AND MORAL STANDARDS? 3

Chapter 2: NATIONALISM:
　　　　　　THE PURE AND SUPERIOR RACE 7

Chapter 3: DISCRIMINATION, APARTHEID,
　　　　　　REFUGEES, AND FOREIGN AID 14

Chapter 4: ALL IS FAIR IN LOVE, WAR AND BUSINESS 19

Section II: **How And Why The Japanese Succeed In Business** ... 30

Chapter 5: PROTECTIONISM REALLY WORKS—
　　　　　　WITH THE HELP OF GATT 31

Chapter 6: PATIENCE, PATIENCE, IS REALLY DELAY, DELAY 44

Chapter 7: HOW TO CAPTURE MARKETS
　　　　　　THE JAPANESE WAY 49

Chapter 8: HOW TO COMPROMISE PEOPLE,
　　　　　　COMPANIES AND GOVERNMENTS 54

Chapter 9: THE JAPANESE LONG RANGE PLAN 61

Section III: *How We Can Still Win The War After Losing So Many Battles* 67

Chapter 10: TOUGHENING GOVERNMENT OFFICIALS AND COUNTERING THE GROWING JAPAN LOBBY 68

Chapter 11: THE JAPANESE ARE NOT PERFECT: LET'S LEARN FROM THEIR MISTAKES 73

Chapter 12: DEALING WITH—AND MAKING DEALS WITH—THE JAPANESE 78

Chapter 13: PROTECTING AND DEVELOPING OUR MANUFACTURING INDUSTRIES 98

Section IV: *The Difficult—But Simple—Solutions All Americans Can Take Part In* 108

Chapter 14: WHAT THE GOVERNMENT CAN DO— IF WE FORCE IT 109

Chapter 15: WHAT BUSINESSES CAN DO 120

Chapter 16: WHAT WE THE PEOPLE CAN DO 130

EPILOGUE 143

Foreword

MANY BOOKS AND articles have been written and will be written about how the United States has lost its competitiveness, quality and manufacturing base and is becoming like an old style colony—**exporting raw materials and importing manufactured goods.**

The great economists and financial experts will give us chapter and verse on the causes.

Our government officials, elected and appointed, will keep telling us they are getting the trade and budget deficit under control only to find after two or three good months disaster will strike again.

The Japanese, Koreans and Taiwanese keep telling us all the great steps they are taking to reduce their trade surplus with the U.S.A. by reducing exports to the U.S.A. and opening their markets so we can trade freely with them only to learn later it was a myth.

Some of our leaders extol the great benefits of the U.S.A. becoming a service economy and getting rid of all those tough and sometimes dirty manufacturing jobs of making steel, ships, castings, cars, TV's, radios, chemicals, etc., etc.

They forget to tell us these service jobs, while very necessary to some degree, pay only $4 to $5 per hour instead of the $10 to $30 per hour.

They also forget to tell us that when we stop manufacturing, we also lose all those other support and downstream jobs of mining, refining, components, services, etc. For example, when General Motors and Toyota set up a joint venture in Fremont,

California, to make cars, over 75% of the parts were imported. Yet, it was called a U.S.A. **manufacturing** plant. It was really only an assembly plant for Japanese components! I wonder who is fooling whom.

We have all been brainwashed into thinking we no longer can make a high quality product in the U.S.A. In fact, our foreign competitors spend untold millions to be sure that we keep getting that message through the media, advertising and lobbyists.

We have all been naive in recognizing what is happening to us and how much worse things will get in the future. Of course, when you think of all the time we spend watching TV and going to the shopping malls to reduce our savings and increase our trade deficit, we don't have much time to think.

I have come to the conclusion that we should not expect much help from our government officials. Unless they change their viewpoints, many of them seem perfectly willing to compromise themselves so they get high paying lobbying jobs with the Japanese when they leave the government.

We cannot expect much help from many of our American businessmen unless they wake up and change their views. Many of them just sit in the U.S.A. "fat and happy" and don't even try to compete in the world markets or improve their quality or service.

It appears that some of our best hope comes from "We the People". This will be discussed in a later chapter.

First, we must know and understand our problems with Japan. What kind of people are we dealing with? What is their long range plan for "world economic domination"? What can the plan lead to? This may sound quite dramatic. But we must put ourselves in the position of the Japanese who show by their actions their determination to dominate much of the world. You recognize the pattern. The old 'co-prosperity sphere.' First they took over Manchuria, Korea, then most of China, all of SE Asia, and later attacked the U.S.A. Now it's economic, not military.

In recent years, I have become more and more concerned about the changing Japanese attitude. The signs of the old Japanese culture and ambitions are starting to emerge. We see more evidence that things are not what we thought they were.

We must be able to recognize the meaning and ulterior motives of the Japanese. We must beware of the smooth talk of their government officials and lobbyists—public statements designed to confuse yet pacify.

We see similar acts of deception like the morning of December 7, 1941, when the Japanese officials were still negotiating in Washington while the Zero's and bombers had left the decks of the carriers to start the bomb run on Pearl Harbor.

We see the increasing Japanese arrogance and superior attitudes toward Americans and Europeans. We see the rise of Nationalism in Japan—the pure and superior race attitude. We see attempts to hide their past from their children and the world by rewriting the Japanese school books. We even see such a distinguished businessman like Akita Morita of Sony cooperate with Shintaro Ishihara in the hate filled book *The Japan That Can Say No*. You begin to realize that the old Japanese attitude of quiet contempt toward foreigners is rising once again.

We hear the former Prime Minister Nakasone make racial slurs against Mexicans, Blacks and Hispanics in America. And we realize that we are once again under attack because we are **not** Japanese and we won't let them have their way with us. Because we question some of their actions, we are called "Japan Bashers."

Prestowitz, Fallows, Burnstein and Karel von Wolferen are some of the most knowledgeable writers on Japan. They have all written excellent books. *More Like Us* by Fallows, a former Carter Administration speech writer; *Trading Places* by Prestowitz, a former U.S. Trade Negotiator; *Yen* by Burnstein, an excellent journalist and writer; *The Enigma of Japanese Power* by Karel van Wolferen, a study of the inner workings of Japan's political/

industry system. The Japanese call them the "Gang of Four" in Japan because they muddy the picture Japan wishes to present to the world. They haven't reacted to Pat Choate's book, *Agents of Influence*, but when they do he will become one of the "Gang of Five."

We watch the Japanese hire high U.S. Government officials as soon as they leave government to lobby for them just to be sure the U.S. Government does what the Japanese want. Some people think the Japanese have more influence over our trade legislation than the administration and our elected Congressmen.

These modern day "Benedict Arnolds" are paid great sums of money by Japan and are among the most powerful in Washington. According to Pat Choate *(Agents of Influence)* the total payment for influencing and brainwashing Americans is about $400,000,000 per year.

When you read this book, please keep in mind that it is written by a plain, ordinary American businessman who spent over 40 years working with, selling to, and competing against our Japanese "friends" in the international markets. The story is of the real world happenings and lessons.

First, a little personal history. I have been working with the Japanese since 1947 as an engineer involved in building Haneda International Airport (Tokyo-Yokohama). I helped set up and was responsible for our most successful joint venture in Japan for 15 years and later involved with our companies other ventures. Over these 40+ years, I made 100 trips to Japan and lived there twice for over three years. I have dealt with all types of Japanese and Japanese companies in Japan, SE Asia and the rest of the world.

I have nothing but praise and admiration for most of the Japanese people I have known over the past 44 years.

The operation which I was responsible for in Japan was the most successful our company had anywhere in the world. The employees were outstanding. The dealings with our 50%

partner were excellent. We did encounter a number of problems but the Japanese hadn't erected enough barriers in time to keep our products out. And we bypassed the traditional distribution systems.

Our two Japanese competitors effectively went out of business because of a simple mistake they made—the same one most U.S. companies make—**they didn't go global soon enough**—and then it is too late.

Most people are truly impressed with the warm and courteous way they are treated by the Japanese. On an individual basis I believe it is quite sincere, but yet you never really get to know most Japanese. But after you work with them for some years, particularly on a business basis, you start to see another side. In our joint venture we basically had a good honest and respectful relationship with a common goal.

Also, after hearing the horror stories of people in other joint ventures, it appeared that our joint venture was quite unique. Probably because we had a good understanding before we started and the secret—all the key people who made the joint venture worked closely with it for fifteen years. Any serious problem could be solved quickly by a meeting of these key people from the two parent companies.

Please remember we are competing against some of the best educated, hardest working nationalistic people on earth. My impression is that their devotion and dedication is to their country first, company second, and family last. This is something most Americans cannot understand, as our priorities are just the opposite!

Their willingness to sacrifice, work hard, think long term and DRIVE, DRIVE, DRIVE is incomprehensible to many modern day Americans. Yet, it was many of the same attributes, but more individualistic in our early Americans that made America great.

So, unless we face up to the problems ahead and take the necessary steps, "They will Win" and "We will Lose." The choice is ours.

Probably for the first time in the history of our country, your children will not live as well as you or your parents. But hopefully, your grandchildren will, if we start taking the necessary steps now.

Without a strong manufacturing base in a broad range of industries, our country will fall back into the status of a developing country. Once you lose this manufacturing base, which is happening, you lose all those related worker skills. Once that happens, it becomes more and more difficult to rebuild the manufacturing base.

We all appreciate that when the Japanese announce they are building an automobile assembly plant or a television plant in the U.S.A. that it is usually not a manufacturing plant. More often it is what we call a "screwdriver plant." That is, a plant where we assemble Japanese parts with a screwdriver.

In most of the Japanese auto plants in America, all the items made with high skills or technology are made in Japan or at a satellite plant in Asia and shipped to the U.S.A. for assembly into the Japanese car. That is currently true with every Japanese transplant with the possible exception of one Honda model which is reported to be 70% American. According to Owen Beiber, President of the United Auto Workers, in 1990, only 38% of the parts used at the Japanese Auto transplants were made in North America. ☐

INTRODUCTION

I HOPE THIS book will open the eyes of our government officials, educators, businessmen and labor leaders and all of middle America.

The idea for this book has been in my mind for years. Strangely, the man who motivated me to write this book is a person whose name I don't even know. It occurred at the US-Asia Conference in Washington, D.C. on February 19, 1986. This was a high level conference of ambassadors and important officials from Southeast Asian countries, top U.S. government officials, U.S. trade officials and other key government and business leaders. At the end of the morning session, we heard wonderful positive comments by Asian officials on how they were opening markets to the U.S.A. and a more negative assessment by U.S. Ambassador Alan Woods, Deputy U.S. Trade Representative. During the question period that followed, all questions were very polite and friendly. None of the questions really got to the core of the problem. I guess this is what we have all been taught at our leading business schools—"never rock the boat if you want to get ahead."

But Ambassador Woods did "rock the boat" when he stated during the question and answer period, that he was most disappointed in the progress of his talks with Japan and, at the current rate, it would take 80 years to resolve our trade differences. He had just spent 4 months to solve 0.6% of the current problems.

The Japanese ambassador made no meaningful comments to his statement.

At this point, and in view of Ambassador Woods' remarks, I

felt the time had come to ask a **real** question. It proved to be an embarrassing question as follows: "Mr. Moderator, I cannot understand why it was taking so long to make any progress since Ambassador Woods has many tools and weapons at his disposal." For example; Since the Japanese have put a 20% duty on plywood imports to Japan, why don't we put a similar duty on Japanese cars? I am confident that if we took such action, Ambassador Woods would find that very serious negotiations would soon develop with Japan."

The response I got from the Moderator was a flippant one: "Well, I am afraid that if we did that, Mr. Conor, all that would happen is that all the Japanese car dealers in America would be angry with us." **Period. End of Subject.**

The Catch 22 of American-Japanese relations, according to those who believe nothing can be done to change Japanese behavior, had struck again. That argument states that if we tick off the Japanese and the Americans who are in tight with them, we will have:

- Angry U.S. business people who are distributors, etc. of Japanese goods;
- Angry U.S. lobbyists for the Japanese, whose fat paychecks have come from a decade or more of being able to twist Congressional arms into not fighting the Japanese;
- Angry U.S. consumers, who can no longer buy Japanese consumer goods which they have been brainwashed into believing are higher quality and less expensive than other — especially American goods;
- Angry Japanese, who will no longer invest in our national debt by buying U.S. government bonds, thereby causing interest rates to rise, which might lead to a recession, thereby lowering consumer demand, thereby ...
- Angry Japanese business people who will begin to lose their greatest market.

But on the other hand there would be:
- Happy American business people and workers whose products would sell better (provided, of course, that they put in the necessary effort to provide good products which they are now doing);
- Happy American farmers who may begin to see the Japanese open their markets to American commodities;
- Happy American workers and their labor unions who would be back at work making products for America;
- Happy Japanese consumers, who have been abused by the Japanese government/industry policies that have kept in place barriers to foreign goods at fair prices in the Japanese markets.

A few minutes later, as we were getting ready to go to lunch, the distinguished gentleman, whom I mentioned above, came up to me and made a very significant statement. "Do you realize, Mr. Conor, you are the only person in this room who dared ask the type of question you did?." I said, "I don't understand." He said, "Well, just stop and think. Not a single lawyer would ask that question as he either has a big Japanese client or is looking for one; there was not a single banker who would ask that question as he either has an important Japanese depositor or is looking for one; there is not a single person in the advertising, media or lobbying business who would dare ask that question because they have large Japanese clients, or are looking for them. There was probably not a single government official who would dare ask that question because he either has a new Japanese factory in his area or is looking for one. So, reflect on this. You are probably the only one who would dare ask such a question. And that is because you must be the only one who is not compromised, as all the others are, even though some may not realize it." So, whoever that person is, I owe him for his revealing analysis. He clearly explained the true source and cause of many of our trade problems with Japan.

I hope that after reading *Japan's New Colony—America*, more people will have the nerve to ask the question I have asked or a question that is similarly pointed. I hope that after reading *Japan's New Colony—America*, people will understand just how we in America have become compromised by Japan, why we must not compromise ourselves, and how we might rebuild America again.

Japan's New Colony—America, is not a book of "mindless Japan bashing" but rather one that exposes and puts into context many facts about the Japanese and their practices Americans either have not been told about or have not listened to because of the pressure and predominance of the Japan lobby and our own "fat and happy" attitude. I feel strongly that after America has reasserted itself it can work not only with Japan, but with all of Asia and Europe to create a more open, democratic, and prosperous world. I also firmly believe that is not the Japanese goal and that if we are to create that kind of relationship, we will **have to force the Japanese into it.** Forcing the Japanese often means taking positions that are unpopular and may even cause short-term pain but I am sure it will entail long-term gain for us and our children. We need to remember that when we deal with the Japanese, we are dealing with some of the best educated, hardest working, and most dedicated people in the world.

And that is really the crux of it; we must start thinking of our relationship with Japan as a long-term endeavor; the Japanese have no real sense of time pressure, so they do everything in the long term. As long as American consumers, producers and government officials fear a "trade war" with the Japanese (I prefer to call it a demand for reciprocal and fair trade policies) we will continue to allow the Japanese to expand their domination and tighten their stranglehold on the American marketplace. I don't think, that faced with real reciprocal pressure, the Japanese would give up the $50 billion annual surplus in exports they generate with the United States. Instead, they will change their business practices. They are much too smart to enter into a trade war since they would lose a surplus of $50 billion a year. But in the process we will get a lot of "American Bashing."

In many ways, we are becoming a colony of Japan; we ship raw materials such as cotton, timber and minerals as well as technological know-how and get back finished consumer goods [it happened in cars, steel, machine tools, consumer electronics, more recently in semi-conductor technology, and is beginning to happen in biotechnology, (which is increasingly becoming the raw material of the high-tech pharmaceutical, chemical and agricultural businesses.)]

I predict that within 10 years we will hear the same kind of repercussions about Japan that we now hear about Iraq—"Why did we (Government and Business, etc.) help them get so strong? Now they are our enemy."

Japan's New Colony—America puts forward a realistic, easy-to-understand plan for Mr. and Mrs. Producer and Mr. and Mrs. Consumer to lead the fight for a more equitable, mutually beneficial, and long-term economic relationship between America and Japan by putting pressure on the Japanese Government and businesses and the American government and businesses.

In the following chapters I will explain why **all is fair in love, war and business.**

You will see why the Japanese failed in their attack on Pearl Harbor. They had no viable follow-up plan.

But they have learned. Now, they think long term and their new attack on the rest of the world is much better planned. And it is long term with well planned follow through.

Their use of GATT rules and various other devices to keep imports out of their country is beautifully executed and lets them develop their industries until they are strong enough to compete.

Their long range plan to take over area markets, build a war chest and attack the next market isn't nice—but it is very effective.

The way they have infiltrated our government, businesses, educational institutions and media to compromise so many people is brilliant.

I have noticed that when I have raised this subject of compromise in speeches over the past several years, a deathly silence has ensued. Apparently, when people examine their own consciences, they realize that they are among the **compromised.**

In the last chapters of this book, I will suggest some solutions to our problems. The solutions are simple and yet difficult. But they are not impossible if the American people understand the problem.

We don't need any government legislation to solve most of the problems. **"We the People"** can do it ourselves ... just like Eastern Europe in 1989. However, as you will note, we could use more intelligence, common sense and backbone in our government, business and labor. ◻

Section I:

What You Really Ought To Know About The Japanese

FIRST OF ALL we should not try to change Japanese culture and customs but we should try to understand them and their strengths and weaknesses and how to deal with them.

Their strengths are well known. Not only have the Japanese made a massive effort to make these strengths known, but their "hirelings"—the lobbyists, the media, the Japanese car dealers and many other well meaning people have helped them. Their education, work habits and dedication to excellence, and related stories are told over and over, but what about their weaknesses?

I presume you might ask why am I, a plain American businessman, qualified to comment on Japanese weaknesses. I may be one of the more qualified with my 44 years of experience in working and competing with them in Japan and around the world.

Having watched our two strong Japanese competitors go out of business also gives me some courage to comment. Also, by understanding their weaknesses and strengths, we made our ventures in Japan more successful. So it's not theory—it's fact.

In the following chapters I will explain some of these Japanese weaknesses in more detail. This will give you an interesting insight into the Japanese character.

As the Japanese keep telling us over and over they are quite different from most other people in the world. They would like us to think this is their high level of education, dedication to work, perfection in manufacturing etc. Most of that is quite true but that is not what makes them different as we see many of those characteristics in other people in the world.

What really makes the Japanese quite different is their strong nationalism. This nationalism isn't the kind we see in some of the Dictator controlled countries. But, as has been explained by some of their Prime Ministers and other high officials, it is due to their conception that they are a superior race. This makes their country much stronger and smarter since, as Prime Minister Nakasone said in September 1986, "The level of intelligence in the United States is lower because of a considerable number of blacks, Puerto Ricans and Mexicans" and because Japan is a one-race society. (He often refers to Japan as monoracial in his speeches.) Unfortunately, Prime Minister Nakasone, the former Minister of Justice, Mr. Kajiyama, and Mr. Ishihara, Author of **The Japan That Can Say No** have, by their remarks, turned nationalism into a racial issue.

This feeling of being superior leads to many of the other Japanese traits and actions. It's something like almost being God. This is quite understandable when your Emperor for hundreds of years was considered to be a God.

So with their different ethical and moral standards, they discriminate against those not of their pure race, and All is Fair in Love, War and Business. They do it because they think they are superior.

In the next four chapters I hope to give you a better insight into the Japanese—not as an intellectual study but as observations by someone who knows them in the real world.

I feel it is most important to analyze the culture, the attitude and actions of the Japanese over the past years (as will be noted in Section I and II) so that we can understand the motives behind the current and future actions of Japan. The things the Japanese are doing today to gain world economic domination follow many of the same basic patterns that we have seen in their past.

It was fortunate that during my many years of working in the international business world, I kept careful notes of my experiences in 109 steno books—"which I never leave home without." ◻

Chapter 1:

WHAT JAPANESE ETHICAL AND MORAL STANDARDS?

I LEARNED EARLY in working in Japan that you had to be careful not to look the other way or you would be put into a position where you had to take a firm stand or your principles would be compromised.

During my first week in Japan in 1947 with the Tokyo Area Engineers, when we were building the International Airport at Haneda, I was asked to approve the Japanese worker payroll for payment. Since I had only been there one week, I really didn't know how to check it—but it did look like a lot of hours work for each person. So I asked my Japanese assistant if she could show me her name on the payroll (it was all in Japanese). With great embarrassment she pointed to her name. It showed about 50% more hours than she had worked. I refused to approve the payroll and great problems ensued. A few weeks later I noticed that one Japanese contractor kept showing a large number of workers on several projects he was working on, but the projects didn't seem to progress very rapidly. I secretly spotted observers near the projects. Alas, they were leap frogging workers from project to project, so as our supervisor came by he could certify the number on the job. Unknown to him they were the same workers he had counted on one of the other projects.

Some time later, we had a problem with a drainage ditch at the airport—the water ran the wrong way! After complaining to this very large contractor (still well known today), the president of the firm tried to convince me it was o.k. ... why not come to his party at Kamachi Inn, etc., etc., etc.

He did redo the ditch—I guess he didn't realize that my school had taught me duty—honor—country and don't let yourself be compromised. So I learned very early about ethics in Japan and how they try to compromise people.

I can recount dozens of similar stories but it all boils down to one thing about the Japanese which I learned from a Japanese colleague. One day I commented about all of the little things Japanese did that I found ethically and morally repugnant. "Most Westerners were brought up to know and understand the Ten Commandments, and most of you try to follow them," he said. "But in Japan, we have no Ten Commandments and we look at things quite differently."

These different ethical and moral standards of the Japanese keep showing themselves over and over.

Now that we look back at World War II and the recent Gulf War, we note that Iraq treated our prisoners of war fairly well compared to how the Japanese treated them during WWII. The Japanese apparently had no respect for the Geneva Convention —and, of course, this resulted in the war crime trials that have been all but hushed up.

While we all know about the Nuremberg war crime trials, very little is known about the Tokyo war crime trials which lasted about three times as long. In fact, they have had so little attention they are almost unknown. Fortunately, Arnold Brackman in his book, *The Other Nuremberg—The Untold Story of the Tokyo War Crime Trials*, gives his first hand report on the trials and the horrible war crimes equal to those of the Germans.

Some years ago I saw an excellent television documentary on how the Japanese mistreated and killed so many of our prisoners of war. It has apparently been banned from TV or maybe the Japanese bought and destroyed it. Who knows??

The killing of some 30,000 U.S. prisoners in the 90 mile Bataan Death March in April 1942, is too horrible to discuss. The treatment of civilian women and children in the Santo Tomas Prison Camp in the Philippines wasn't much better.

The way they treated the Koreans during their many years of occupation reminds you of the Iraqi occupation of Kuwait. Keeping the Koreans from getting educated in Science and Engineering was one more way to subdue a race. The rape of Nanking in December 1937, where the Japanese killed from 100,000 to 300,000 civilians and POW's in a few weeks shows that such behavior was almost endemic. And now they try to deny it ever happened. Particularly vocal on this subject is Diet Member Shintaro Ishihara (the author of the book *The Japan Can Say No* with Mr. Morita, Chairman of Sony—Mr. Morita was not associated with the book when it was republished in America in 1990) who was quoted as saying in a *Playboy* magazine interview, "The Rape of Nanjing" is nothing more than "... a story made up by the Chinese. The Chinese People's Daily responded by saying "Lies cannot obscure facts written in blood." Despite all this the Japanese government says nothing. Maybe they agree with Ishihara?

I was in Hong Kong a few years ago when I saw the first Chinese reaction to the Japanese rewriting of their textbooks to ensure their students never learned about the Rape of Nanjing (or Nanking as it was previously called). That Sunday the local Chinese bombed the Japanese department store Matsuzakaya, and held a major demonstration against Japan, with 30,000 protesters in Victoria Park. At that same time, the Chinese government in Beijing canceled their invitation to the Japanese Minister of Education to visit China. The Chinese have continued these protests but Japan still makes sure their young people never learn about Japan's past.

When a country or their people cannot admit their actions or mistakes it could mean that they saw nothing wrong in their past actions!!

It is particularly disturbing when a Member of the Diet (and some say a possible future Prime Minister) can say today in the 1990's that these horrible events never happened.

The past events have been removed or so downgraded in the Japanese textbooks that the young people think it was Western propaganda.

So there is a serious question about what kind of ethical and moral standards exist in Japan.

Even though Japan has treated most Asians as second class citizens, or worse, for years—they still run big sex tours for the men to those same Southeast Asian countries.

The ulterior motives behind many Japanese actions seem to be unnoticed by most Americans or they are afraid to comment lest they be called "Japan Bashers". Recently, however, we see a few of these Japanese actions slipping into the news. Such as the Branch Manager at the Bank of California (owned by Mitsubishi) being awarded $6.3 million by the court for being dismissed because he blocked attempts by Mitsubishi to get key confidential financial information on the bank's customers. This apparently is a routine practice by some Japanese companies who buy U.S. companies.

Recently, one of my friends in the consulting business who has a Japanese client was invited by his client to meet the President of a Japanese Bank. I understand this was a rare event as the Bank's President didn't like to meet foreigners.

During the meeting, the Japanese client (who was a close friend of the Bank President) mentioned he was having some difficulty with some officials in Washington. Without hesitation, the Bank President said, "We'll just buy them off and get the job done." It was quite clear that this was standard operating procedure.

This really shouldn't surprise anyone except for the fact that he never even for a moment considered any other approach to solve the problem. As I have said before, "All is fair in love, war and business" to many Japanese.

And if greedy Americans can be bought—buy them. □

Chapter 2:

NATIONALISM: THE PURE AND SUPERIOR RACE

I DO NOT intend my comments on Japan to focus on race but rather Nationalism. Unfortunately, since Japan prides itself on being a nation of a pure race, the words Race and Nationalism mean the same to most people. We don't have that problem in America since we are in the words of some Japanese a "mongrelized race."

Some people may think this chapter refers to the Japan of the early 1900's through World War II. That is not the intent. I only refer to that earlier period so that we can understand their actions and culture and how they explain the actions and motives of the Japanese in recent years—and today.

While the exhibitions of their Nationalism may be more subtle today, I feel they are even stronger and more dangerous than in the earlier period.

We are now seeing this Nationalism manifested as a new arrogance—a superior attitude—a smugness that lets the rest of the world know it is inferior.

They tell us on a regular basis, either directly or through their lobbyists and other agents or brainwashed, but well meaning, people that only things Japanese are well made.

It is possible for Japan to send out this clear message as they work in a unified way, not on an individual way as most Americans.

You see this very different approach to life. In America we see our priorities as Family—Company—Country in that order. But in Japan it is quite different—First comes Country—Next Company—and Last Family. All you have to do is to take a late train from Grand Central Station in New York to Westchester on any work day and see that most of the passengers are Japanese businessmen. They have given their all to the Company and Country—and the Family will have to wait!

I would not want to infer by this comment that the Japanese have any less regard for their families—It's only that they must first be sure their Country and Company are most successful.

Also this strong nationalism has no visible effect on their one to one social relations with most foreigners. They are probably the most thoughtful, courteous people you will ever meet.

Unfortunately, this courteous, kind attitude doesn't apply to some of their people such as Prime Minister Nakasone who has probably made the greatest racial slur in history against the minorities in America. The same applies to the remarks of the Japanese Minister of Justice in October 1990, when, after inspecting a police raid on prostitutes operating in the Shinjuku Section of Tokyo, he made a remark, the gist of which went something like this, "Prostitutes ruin a neighborhood in Japan just like blacks ruin a neighborhood in America."

Later, he apologized and resigned. Prime Minister Nakasone still has not apologized for his famous remarks about our minorities.

While you don't feel this strong nationalism in your relations with individuals you do see it in the government policies and actions and the way they control and restrict everything. For example the way they decide which industries will succeed and which ones will not succeed or be moved out of Japan. The way they decide how the people will live—how they will go without or make other sacrifices to make Japan the Superior nation in the world.

I will not attempt to explain this nationalism in great detail but I would urge anyone who wants to better understand Japanese nationalism to read the excellent articles in the magazine *World Press Review* and *The Far Eastern Economic Review*. *World Press*

Review, March 1987—a reprint of an article from Der Spiegel—(Behind Japanese Superiority) which describes in great detail what many of us have seen in Japan for years—the pure superior race—the discrimination against foreigners (especially if you are black) and the other inferior human beings in their mind. In the Far Eastern Economic Review article (19 Feb 1987—Article—"Nakasone's Neo-Nationalism" they explain the heavy racial overtones of Nakasone's speeches which we have heard many times in Japan.

Unfortunately, this other side of Japan is rarely mentioned in American media—I can only assume it's because the Japanese Lobbyists have such control over our media or that they are such big customers of our media they encourage the media not to report such stories or they might lose a customer. Whatever the reason, this information is well censored from the majority of the American people.

You do occasionally see such articles in U.S. Newspapers such as the article in the *New York Times*, April 12, 1987, by Ian Buruma titled "A New Japanese Nationalism."

I was in Japan in September 1986, when Nakasone made his infamous racial remarks at a study session of the Liberal-Democratic Party. He told the meeting that Japan has a higher "Intelligence Level" than the United States because Japan is a one-race society. "The level in the United States is lower because of a considerable number of blacks, Puerto Ricans and Mexicans." This was not surprising to me as most of us who have worked in Japan are aware of this feeling, among many Japanese, not only toward our minorities but also toward most foreigners. The only surprise is that he was so blunt and the story leaked out.

Over the years, most of us who have worked closely with the Japanese had looked upon all these comments and actions by the Japanese as Nationalism. But Nakasone in his many writings and speeches has turned it into a racial issue—which is most unfortunate. You cannot but be reminded of Hitler's similar remarks about the pure superior race.

In the past, Japan has been very subtle in its dealings with foreigners so as not to alarm them with their strong nationalism. But this is changing as they get stronger and stronger economically.

We recently saw a demonstration of this in early 1991 when the United States displayed a sample of American rice at an exhibition in Tokyo. The Japanese Authorities threatened to arrest our people if they did not remove the rice from the exhibition.

Can you imagine what would happen in America if we threatened to arrest anyone who displayed an imported Japanese car? The Japanese would have hired so many U.S. lawyers that the case would probably be all the way to the Supreme Court in weeks!!

We must understand that Japan is no longer playing softball — They are playing **hardball**. This is getting much easier for them as they compromise and brainwash more and more of our local and national government officials, media and educators. This is well explained and documented in Pat Choate's book *Agents of Influence*.

You see this again in the original Japanese version of the book *The Japan That Can Say No* (the American version is cleaned up). This book by Mr. Isihara, the DIET Member, and Mr. Morita, the Chairman of Sony, has reached a new high in "America Bashing." It is interesting to note that in the American version of the book, Mr. Morita of Sony disassociated himself from the book. I am sure he understood very well that if Americans knew he supported such thoughts and ideas it might become very difficult to sell Sony products in America. The fact is — that he still wrote part of the original book — so we know his true feeling about us Americans. After reading the original version of their book, I realized that there never has been a "Japan Basher" who could possibly do such a great job of bashing a country as Isihara and Morita have done in their book.

Once you understand this powerful Japanese nationalism, it is easy to explain many of their current actions. You realize why they rewrite history in their textbooks, why they censor American movies like "The Last Emperor" all to be sure their children can think of themselves as a country who never did anything bad.

I regret having to point out all of these unfortunate traits and actions by the Japanese. However unless you understand their past you cannot understand their current actions and motives.

This strong nationalism in Japan has caused me to realize that Japan is the most nationalistic and racist country I have encountered in some 70 or so countries I have worked in around the world.

Yet, at the same time, they call us racist if we say anything about them. Mr. Isihara goes into great lengths on this subject.

You see these examples over and over.

Sometime ago, the Dutch Journalist, Karel van Wolferen wrote a book *The Enigma Of Japanese Power*. The Japanese didn't like this book so it was restricted from sale in Japan. The Japanese called van Wolferen and three other fine writers who had written books on Japan, "The Gang of Four." They had apparently explained a side of Japan that the Japanese didn't want the world to know about. But as is quite normal, it wasn't the Japanese government who restricted the sale of the book in Japan but a distributor. We have seen this many times in the business world when your products are restricted from sale in Japan by some Association (who isn't getting a "kickback" as they get from the Japanese manufacturer), or some safety or minority group, etc. The government hides behind all these excuses and pretends it is not involved. The Japanese think this is very subtle but those of us who have had to deal with the problem think it's quite blatant.

We keep seeing these clandestine actions of Japan—such as buying up the secret software related to our "Star War" programs. Fortunately, the American involved in this was arrested. The Japanese companies involved would like us to believe they didn't realize this was a high level strategic item. "So sorry."

When you appreciate how they analyze every detail of an American market for a product, with great perfection, you wonder how they can be so ignorant as to make racial slurs about our minorities, try to buy our military secrets or sell our secret technology to U.S.S.R. and claim they didn't understand. You soon realize it's like dealing with someone who "talks out of both sides of his mouth."

And there are still more incidents. Take the comment attributed to an official of a major Japanese company who allegedly said, "The Japanese are people who can manufacture a product of uniform and superior quality because the Japanese are a race of pure blood and not the mongrelized race as in the United States."

With so many similar incidents with high Japanese officials over the years, I have come to the conclusion it's not that they don't know what they are doing, it's just that they don't care. You might almost think it's intentional. You don't see them making ignorant mistakes when they want to sell a product in America or influence a government action in Washington.

Japanese nationalism rears its ugly head in many ways but the most common is the attempt to wipe out the past bad history of Japan.

In 1988, when the movie "The Last Emperor" (the story about China) was shown in Japan, we saw a similar reaction. The Japanese decided that they could not show the movie unless they censored portions that showed the Japanese occupation and rape of China. They gave many excuses for censoring this movie. The key one appears to have been that they felt they had to cut out all portions showing Japanese atrocities in China, since it would cause confusion in the minds of the young people. It certainly would be confusing since it would contradict what was in the Japanese history books on the occupation of China.

We can only wonder what will happen to our movies made at Columbia Pictures and MCA now that they are owned by the Japanese. The new Japanese owners have tried to reassure the American people they will not control the content of the movies made in these U.S. Studios. Judging by Japanese actions in the past you can't help but wonder what kind of freedom the directors and producers will really have in the long run.

When the head of Matsushita, who had just purchased MCA, was asked if they would control the content of new movies, he was very upset for being asked a hypothetical question. He refused to answer the question and said something to the effect that he could not see such a thing ever happening.

We have all heard many comments in the past from the Japanese about what they would or would not do and watched them reverse themselves. We have been to many meetings where the Japanese told us how open their markets are only to find some new barrier. So if you still believe in the "Tooth Fairy" it's okay to believe these Japanese comments. Otherwise, watch out. I think we must all be prepared for future censoring of our movies. It will never be mentioned —you won't hear about it—the producers will not even present a story that would offend the Japanese. They will know that either they will never get the funding for the movie or they may not work there any longer. If the Japanese follow their normal procedures of "Administrative Guidance" it will all happen very quietly. □

Chapter 3:

DISCRIMINATION, APARTHEID, REFUGEES, FOREIGN AID

WHILE MANY PEOPLE have various perceptions of Japan's motives, here we have a chance to see their true thoughts in action. We don't have to speculate or theorize on their motives, we can examine them in practice.

DISCRIMINATION

Discrimination takes many forms in Japan—against women, foreigners and minorities.

This was a revelation to most of us Americans. I soon realized that we had never seen such open discrimination in business. We all understood that women stayed in the back-ground and walked a few paces behind the men, etc., but when a Japanese woman employee who was doing an outstanding job for years in our company, was promoted to a Section Chief (the equal of a small department manager) we learned a new lesson.

Very high level executives of our partners quickly advised me that such things were not done in Japan. This was discussed for some months (with her still keeping the title) on the grounds that she was the most capable person for the job. If they could suggest another person for the job and would take full responsibility for his performance, we would discuss the situation. The issue finally faded away, when we started the discussions on buying the other 50% of the joint venture. Later, when we owned 100% of the former JV she continued in the job.

How women who believe in women's rights can, in good conscience, go out and buy a Japanese car and indirectly support this discrimination is beyond me. Maybe those women really aren't very concerned about women's rights unless it specifically applies to them and not to some other women. They have no idea what an impact they could have on women's rights in Japan if they stopped buying Japanese cars.

As you have probably noted, from time to time the Japanese put out a news story on the great advances of Japanese women. This just illustrates their guilt complex over this problem. Maybe now and then a few women do get a little more recognition.

I put these stories in the same category as the stories of how the Japanese market is an open market and the only reason we don't sell there is that we don't try. When you see the next big shipment of U.S. grown rice sent to Japan, please let me know. Hopefully, it may happen in our lifetime.

There are many examples of how everyone except the Japanese are inferior people and really second class citizens.

Whenever we had a problem with a customer in Japan, such as not paying a bill, the Japanese without hesitation and without finding out who the customer was would say "he must be Korean." It took me a long time to get used to this. But I never understood what real discrimination was until I did some work in Korea and heard their stories about the Japanese occupation.

During the years of the Japanese occupation, they never permitted the Koreans to be educated as engineers. That was one very effective way to keep them down in the rice paddy.

We may be facing a similar treatment as the Japanese take over more and more of our manufactured products—televisions, VCR's, radios, computers, ships, cars, etc., and we become a service economy with no products to sell or export. The new movies and TV shows will be what the Japanese owners of our movie studios want us to see.

APARTHEID

I would not want to leave the impression that I think the Japanese are supporters of apartheid as a principle, but for them to support an apartheid government to get business is all right. Remember, **"All is fair in love, war and business."** Just keep this phrase in mind and you will better understand all the actions of Japan.

When the Americans and many Europeans pulled out of South Africa and some even placed sanctions on business with South Africa, the Japanese saw this as a great business opportunity. As "honorary whites" they were free to move. They were so successful with their exports to South Africa that in six months (increasing over 45%) they became South Africa's largest trading partner. In 1988, Japan's trade with South Africa increased by an estimated 30% to about four times the U.S. trade. The U.S. trade dropped over 50% in the 1980's. At the time, the Japanese sale of computers and other items such as cars by Nissan (a 40% increase) and Toyota (over 80,000 cars) may have violated the 1986 anti-apartheid act. That would have permitted the U.S.A. to impose sanctions against Japan. Nothing happened, so the Japanese hired-guns the lobbyists must have squelched that from happening. Who knows??

The Japanese Trade Ministry Official only said they asked the Japanese exporters to be careful, but there is no law against exports!!

Our United States sanctions became almost meaningless. (Even though our Congress and the media keep discussing the possible removal of sanctions, it would almost be a non-event). (Bush did lift sanctions in July, 1991). The Japanese shipped in thousands of kits to assemble Japanese cars and trucks in South Africa, plus a broad range of other products that we were not allowed to sell.

So, again, I say if you are against apartheid, how can you in good conscience keep driving that Japanese car or, even worse, go out and buy one.

How those college students can have a big protest demonstration about Coca-Cola selling a soft drink to South Africa and then jump in their Japanese car to go to their room to play the Japanese VCR and TV, is somewhat hypocritical. I'm sure if they knew these facts they would act quite differently. It is most unfortunate that these facts about Japan are not better known.

If with this knowledge protestors directed their efforts in a more informed direction, they could have had a great effect on **their** future well being. But the Japanese are even working to be sure that doesn't happen by making generous grants to our universities—and compromising more and more people.

FOREIGN AID

After years of giving almost no foreign aid, except what they were forced to do by some Southeast Asian countries they plundered, the Japanese now crow they are number one aid givers.

What they don't tell you is that almost all their past aid was "tied" aid—i.e. the money could only be spent for Japanese products or services. In effect, it was a way for Japanese companies to invade and take over markets.

In May 1990, I was invited by the Japanese Consulate office in New York to meet with Mr. Hayashi. Mr. Hayashi was a key official in the Japanese Foreign Ministry who was responsible for so called "soft loans". These are very low interest loans to foreign countries which may never be repaid.

I understand the purpose of Mr. Hayashi's visit to the U.S. was to meet with many government officials or business people who had been deeply involved in China to obtain their reactions regarding a proposed large loan to the People's Republic of China. Japan had promised this large loan prior to the Tiananmen Square incident but then postponed granting the loan. The amount of the loan was to be some 5 billion dollars.

Mr. Hayashi was quick to point out that, while in the past many Japanese foreign aid loans were "tied," they had adopted a new policy so that only some of the new loans were "tied." The two other people at the meeting and myself said we saw no problem with the China loan as long as it was not tied and the Chinese were free to spend the money anywhere in the world to do worthwhile projects. I assume he must have received similar reactions elsewhere, as when Prime Minister Kaifo met President Bush in Houston a few weeks later it was announced that Japan would make the loan.

After the two other Americans left the lunch, I passed on to Mr. Hayashi a few other comments and suggestions to improve relations between the U.S. and Japan.

For instance, why did they keep fueling the fire over restrictions on our sale of beef and rice to Japan? It was like shooting themselves in the foot. Why didn't they let us sell them virtually unlimited amounts of rice and beef (like we let them ship us cars) and if it caused them some so called "political problem" they could just give the rice and beef to some poor starving nation. That would be real foreign aid!!

REFUGEES

Japan has a long history of keeping out refugees. They have only agreed to take 10,000 from Southeast Asia, while we took hundreds of thousands, and at last reports, only part of their 10,000 quota was allowed in.

They want to keep their race pure. They apparently have no real concern for the suffering of their neighbors. We all wonder where Japan was during the Kurd Refugee problem in 1991. They probably didn't want to get involved as it might interfere with their future deals with Saddam Hussein for oil. □

Chapter 4:

ALL IS FAIR IN LOVE, WAR AND BUSINESS

WE HAVE ALL seen many examples of the Japanese behavior in all three of these areas— **Love, War and Business**—over the past many years.

I have come to believe that Japanese actions in each of these areas are not isolated incidents but are a part of their culture. An understanding of their behavior in love and war is very important to better understand their behavior in business.

LOVE

It is well known to the world that the Japanese treat their wives in a somewhat subservient manner. We are all quite familiar with the stories that Japanese women walk a few feet behind their husbands, and that Japanese women are rarely included in any social event. Although some of this behavior is changing with younger people, it is still very prevalent in the country. The one element which has bothered westerners a great deal is not only the way that they treat their women as second class citizens but their overall conduct towards women in general. Probably the most notable manifestation of this general attitude are the highly promoted sex tours to the other Asian countries.

WAR

Most of the examples of Japanese behavior in this area are really too terrible to dwell on.
- The Rape of Nanking—an estimated 100-300,000 people killed by the Japanese in a few weeks of terror.
- Bataan Death March—an estimated 30,000 American

prisoners died in a few days on the march from Bataan to the Japanese prison camp in the Philippines.
- Sneak attack on Pearl Harbor—December 7, 1941, While Japanese diplomats were having discussions in Washington, D.C., the Japanese planes were in the air enroute to bomb Pearl Harbor.
- Medical experiments on POW's.

The Japanese still pretend these things never happened, as they are barely mentioned in the current Japanese history books. However, they beat the drums on our bombing of Hiroshima and Nagasaki to **end** the war but they never mention they **started** the war with the sneak attack followed by many horrible crimes. All of these actions and later denials show the strange thought processes that go on in Japanese official minds.

How can they claim our action to end the war is so horrible and their actions starting the war and during the war are completely ignored?

As you stop and review Japanese actions in business dealings they often have similar characteristics. This is the area we will discuss in this book.

BUSINESS

This is where the Japanese actions have been similar but much more subtle. Most of you are probably hearing it for the first time.

Politics, Apartheid, Religion or bribes—none of these things get in the way if the Japanese want the business. Even trading with our enemies, Iran, Vietnam, North Korea is okay for them. This is all routine with the Japanese as **"All is fair in love, war and business."**

An example of how the Japanese approach the fairness in business is almost humorous if it was not so serious.

Several years ago when the U.S.-Japanese Trade Relations were becoming particularly strained, (one of the many times over the last 20 years) the Japanese decided they had to do something. It had to be very visible and very public to explain to America that they were really very nice people and they were really opening up their markets so we could balance our trade. Their solution to this problem and to get maximum publicity was the Nakasone Market Access Promotion Mission. It was a very large mission of many of the top people of Japanese Industry and Government. They put on a large show at the Waldorf Astoria Hotel in New York. The Mission was led by Mr. Yahiro, President of Mitsui and Co. The other leaders were the heads, or key people, in the famous Japanese companies or organizations—Daiei, C. Itoh, Hankyu, Toyo, Kanematsu-Gosho, Japan Automobile Importers Assn., MITI and Ministry of Foreign Affairs Officials.

I was invited by the Japanese to attend the meeting and the lunch preceding the formal meeting. During the lunch, a Foreign Ministry Official asked me what I was going to do when I retired from AMF a few months later. (This was probably my chance to become a highly paid lobbyist). I replied I was thinking of opening a supermarket in Tokyo and selling rice, beef, citrus fruits, cigarettes, etc. and make my fortune. He had a stunned look on his face and said, "That would be very difficult as those items are restricted imports to Japan." I said, "How can that be, Prime Minister Nakasone has assured us that the Japanese market is completely open? In fact, I understood that was one of the main purposes of this great Mission and meeting here in New York."—**Silence.**

Once again, you understand what the Japanese say in public and what they really mean is quite different. Unfortunately, this message has never been given to the American people or at least not in a way that it has been understood. It is also quite clear that our government officials themselves have never understood this Japanese tactic.

Later that day, during the formal meeting in the large hall at the Waldorf, with excellent simultaneous translators and with all the members of the Prime Minister's Market Access Promotion Committee and U.S. officials, we got down to business.

JAPANESE MARKET ACCESS PROMOTION MISSION
Member List

Leader:	Mr. Toshikuno Yahiro, *President*, Mitsui & Co., Ltd.
Deputy Leader:	Mr. Isao Nakauchi, *Chairman, President & CEO* The Daiei, Inc.
	Mr. Hiroshi Kamiya, *Executive Vice President* C. Itoh & Co., Ltd.
	Mr. Tohru Noda, *Vice President* Hankyu Department Store, Inc.
	Mr. Hisashi Nomura, *President* Toyo Corporation
	Mr. Hideo Suzuki, *President* Kanematsu-Gosho, Ltd.
	Mr. Yoshihiro Tajima, *Chairman* Distribution Economics Institute of Japan
	Mr. Jiro Yanase, *President* Japan Automobile Importers Association
Advisor:	President, JETRO
Government Officer:	MITI Official
Officer:	Ministry of Foreign Affairs Official

As the meeting progressed, it became angrier and angrier as one after another U.S. company representative complained how their products were kept out of Japan by a variety of barriers.

We had also heard the great praise, the leader of the mission bestowed on Mr. Yanase (the distributor of G.M. cars in Japan) for importing so many G.M. cars to Japan. (Probably a few hundred). Then just before the end of the meeting with the bitter statements getting stronger and stronger, I made a statement. "I am pleased to hear the great success Mr. Yanase has had in importing G.M. cars. Mr. Yanase has been the distributor of our Hatteras yachts for years, but he has never sold one even though they are sold all over the world. The problem is the horrendous restrictions on importing yachts to Japan." The room became silent. Then I said, "I'm sure that this powerful Mission can solve that problem very quickly. With all the rich and powerful men on the committee I will be waiting outside the door with my order book. The yachts are only about $1 million each."

The whole room broke out with great cheers and applause and the statement had completely diffused the bad atmosphere in the room. But while they knew they had been exposed, the Japanese were pleased to stop the angry statements.

I returned to my office and within an hour the phone rang. It was the Japanese Ambassador's office. They wanted to send a representative to my office to solve the yacht problem.

Once again, my strategy of working with the Japanese to solve a problem had worked—**Embarrass them publicly.**

A few weeks later, I was invited to meet with the Ministry of Transportation in Japan, to finalize the solution to the yacht problem. I was quickly informed that there had been "a big mistake." Those difficult import restrictions were meant to apply to large tankers and very small boats, not the fine Hatteras yachts!! "Touche." Just one more example of how Japan really operates and why we need to say "NO" to Japan.

In conclusion, the "Nakasone Market Access Promotion Committee" was just one more Japanese publicity stunt to influence the American media, and, in turn, influence the American people. But **"All is Fair in Love, War and Business."**

Not only have the Japanese shown how easy it is to keep imported products out of their country, they often do an even better job on services.

One of the most interesting examples is how they handle American Lawyers who try to penetrate their markets.

During my early days of working on the China Market, I became acquainted with a Charles Stevens of the Coudert Brothers law firm, who later headed up their office in Tokyo. It is interesting to note that even though Coudert is a highly respected and well known international law firm, they were not allowed to use their name in Japan. The same was true of all foreign law firms. The Japanese have special rules regulating various foreign services. The rule regarding law firms is that you can't use your firm's name but you must use the name of the senior lawyer in the firm in Japan. This means that one day your firm may be called Stevens, and after he leaves the new name may be Jones—then Simpson, etc. It does a wonderful job of eliminating name recognition.

Can you just imagine what would happen in America if we treated the Japanese in a similar manner? One day Nomura Securities would be Nomura if a Mr. Nomura was the local head of the firm. Then when he leaves and goes back to Japan and Mr. Saito heads up the firm it would have to be renamed Saito Securities. Then later Ishihara Securities. Can you just imagine the complaints we would get from Japan if we treated the Japanese as they treat us?

But we are just "patsies" and let them get away with anything they want so they can proceed with their plan to dominate the world.

Stealing IBM Secrets—IBM accused the Japanese of stealing their secrets. I happened to be in Japan in 1983 when it was announced that the criminal case against Hitachi and the other IBM actions against Mitsubishi and Fujitsu had been settled. While the details of this deal were kept secret, it was disclosed that some Japanese computer manufacturers would not only make large payments to IBM but they would permit IBM, some months before a new computer was put on the market, the opportunity to inspect the equipment to ensure it did not contain any IBM secrets.

As I was reading the paper that morning, I noticed in the article a sub headline "National Disgrace." I thought to myself isn't that great the Japanese publicly admit they stole the IBM secrets and the country is embarrassed. But as I read further in the article, I realized the headline had an entirely different meaning. It was not a "National Disgrace" that they had been caught. It was a "National Disgrace" that they had to show IBM their new equipment before it was put on the market!!

But **"All is Fair in Love — War and Business."** This just gives you a little insight into the Japanese mind.

Chip Technology — Here again we see the Japanese approach to how you use someone else's patented technology so you can become dominate in the world. In 1960, Texas Instruments, who owned the key patent for virtually all integrated circuits, applied for the patent in Japan. The Japanese took **29 years** to grant the patent. In the meantime, Japan developed the largest chip industry in the world apparently using stolen technology.

As you can see, you have to constantly keep your guard up as they have all kinds of ways to work around any restriction you may put on them.

Beef — Some years ago, the Japanese had a quota on U.S. beef limiting our sales to 40,000 tons per year. At the same time, I learned from some friends in Australia that the Japanese let them export 80,000 tons of beef to Japan.

At my next meeting with MITI Officials, I asked the Japanese how come we can only ship you 40,000 tons and the Australians can ship you twice as much. Oh, Mr. Conor, we have a big problem. The Australians told us that if we wanted to buy bauxite from Australia, we had to buy more beef. So we bought more beef. But our government is weak. We don't demand fair trade with Japan.

Other Import Restrictions — Some time ago, I was transferring one of our people to our company in Japan to better qualify him in international business and strengthen our Japanese office.

He asked if we would approve the shipment of his new Audi 4000 to Japan. We agreed and asked him to get permission from the Japanese to bring in his own private car. We agreed to pay transportation and other costs to bring his car to Japan. We assumed the other costs would be nominal since it was a fine German car that was almost new and it met all the American standards.

He went to the Japanese import authorities and was advised that unfortunately the German car was not too well made. It would require about $3,500 of modifications. The entire electrical system would have to be replaced plus several other items to make it acceptable to Japanese standards. (But it would **not** be necessary to move the steering wheel from the left to the right side.) It would also take several months to get this work done.

With these restrictions, we gave him an okay to buy a cheap Japanese car. In the overall picture, this is a very small item but it illustrates the lengths the Japanese will go to protect their market from imports.

That year the Japanese shipped to America about 600,000 cars and they didn't have to get them inspected after arrival in the U.S.A. We accepted their word that they met U.S. regulations.

These are just a few of the little trip ropes that cause you to stumble along the way in trying to do business in Japan. But **"All is Fair in Love, War and Business."**

Other Policy Issues

Despite being a member of the Coordinating Committee on Multilateral Exports (COCOM), which coordinated and sanctioned trade with Eastern Europe before the political openings of 1989-1990, Japanese companies routinely allowed sophisticated technology to go to the Eastern Bloc. But again in 1989, we hear that Japan illegally shipped high tech equipment made by Canon for computer chip manufacturers to East Germany via Korea. The Japanese government apparently did nothing to stop it, even assisting companies to overcome the bad publicity. It gave Japan a foothold in another market. Politics and rules be damned.

Toshiba—Exports Secret to Soviets—Toshiba Machinery Co. illegally exported, in violation of the regulations of COCOM (Coordinating Committee of Multilateral Export Controls), sophisticated machinery for making submarine propellers to the Soviet Union.

Needless to say, our Congress was very upset and we did restrict the sales of some Toshiba products for a short time. But it just illustrates once again the Japanese will sell to anyone to make a profit—and the Japanese government does very little to control such actions.

So we do have to question the real attitude of Japan in business. But **"All is Fair in Love, War and Business."**

Japan continues to fight spending more money on defense, instead using its economic muscle to claim new markets while the United States pays for world defense. In addition, few Americans have understood that American defense of oil tankers in the Persian Gulf did not really guarantee supply to the United States—a small portion of our oil came from Iran and Iraq—but, rather, it guaranteed uninterrupted supply to Japan.

Now that we have had Desert Shield and Desert Storm, with Japan again it's a case of "promises, promises," but little action. The Japanese should be ashamed of themselves—but we are the suckers to let them get away with us protecting their supply sources while they scheme to take over the American economy.

They just can't help themselves. It must be a part of their culture as we look back over their actions in Mongolia, Korea, China, WWII, etc.

Then again in 1991, Senator Lloyd Bentsen asked for a report by the General Accounting Office on allegations made in a report by the Commerce Department and comments by Sematech that Japanese manufacturers of advanced equipment for making chips were withholding the sale of equipment to U.S. firms.

The Japanese, of course, will deny this even though it is true. They will have dozens of explanations. But these illegal actions by the Japanese go on day after day. As they get more powerful and more arrogant they seem to be less concerned.

The Examples of Unfair Play Continue

Here in 1991, we see NEC (Nippon Electric Corp.) agreeing to pay the U.S. Government $34 million for bid rigging on a contract to supply communication equipment to U.S. bases in Japan.

Then a few days later we see Nippon Steel agreeing to pay Allegheny Ludlum Corp. several million dollars for infringing on Allegheny patents for several years.

At least we Americans are getting more aggressive and forcing the Japanese companies to pay up for cheating.

But this problem of stealing our technology may sadly come to an end. A friend of mine, who knows I am writing this book, sent me a note about a comment he had heard. It went something like this, "We have been concerned that the Japanese have stolen our technology. They are concerned that there may be nothing left to steal."

In spite of all this, I have seen one small grain of hope in Japan from some of the younger men.

I was surprised one day while at a farewell party for a young Japanese Foreign Ministry Official. He explained to me that he was greatly concerned that his government and businesses in Japan were over playing their hand on exports. They were pushing too hard and not listening to what was being said around the world. He was concerned that when the old guard passed away and he and the other younger men took over, they would be faced with some very serious backlash.

His is just one voice crying in the wilderness. But don't expect anything to happen unless "We the People" make it happen.

I am sure the Japanese Government Officials are so confident of their control of our government officials and the media, and the power of their broad network of lobbyists, that they can keep this under control and avoid a backlash. ◻

Section II:

How And Why The Japanese Succeed In Business

IN THE FIVE *chapters in this section, I'll describe my conception of the Japanese plan for world economic domination—protect markets at home until businesses and industries become strong then help them capture markets abroad. Talk as much as anyone wants about opening Japanese markets, but continue to build the protective maze of regulations, specifications and "guidance" that make it impossible for anyone but one of the inside players to be successful.*

*I'll describe about how Americans have become compromised by the Japanese. How in our rush to become partners—and good partners at that—we have really been pushed further and further up against the wall so that our **partners really control us.***

Just like colonies, entire classes of people—business people, lawyers, lobbyists, advertising, public relations professionals, former congressmen and trade negotiators, and even journalists and media companies—are being created who owe their financial existence, often at six and even seven-figure salaries, commissions or lobbying fees to the good graces of the Japanese. ☐

Chapter 5:

PROTECTIONISM REALLY WORKS— WITH THE HELP OF GATT

THE ITEMS NOTED in this chapter cover the most visible areas of difficulty with Japan—**Protectionism.**

The Japanese like to present a picture that **protectionism** is a terrible practice. Their lobbyists and hirelings put out all kinds of news articles on the terrible results of **protectionism.**

Yet, Japan is the world master of **protectionism.** When we comment on their **protectionism,** we are "Japan Bashers."

The articles that have been written on this subject by Japanese and Americans would cover thousands of pages.

This subject has been the cause of more debates and arguments and differences between us and Japan than probably any other single item.

Over the last 30 years that I have followed this subject, and been deeply involved in it, the Japanese, on at least 100 occasions, have promised us their markets are being opened and we can ship them any product. Then a little later after each announcement we hear the details. The duty of say 40% will be reduced by one-half over the next 20 years. Or 100 items are opened for import only to learn that most of the items are of no interest to most exporters or the market is too small in Japan to be considered.

Even when the item is really freed for import, we learn later of other downstream restrictions, such as so called safety seals, approval of product after arrival in Japan, unusual specifications, etc. The barriers keep cropping up.

These Japanese announcements make very good press but offer very little substance. They can plant these stories so well in our media that most Americans really believe them. The skill of the Japanese in this area is outstanding.

This whole program of how to keep products out of Japan, to protect their industries, and at the same time keep the atmosphere cool enough in America so they can ship here uninhibited is probably one of their greatest accomplishments. I have never seen the Japanese do anything as brilliantly as they have in keeping their markets closed and our markets open.

Their excuses have changed a lot over the years but very little has changed about really opening their markets.

Our trade deficit has kept climbing. We ship them $20 billion of materials, they ship us $70 billion of manufactured goods. Sure they have made some modest publicity concessions to allow a few more things to come in, but the Japanese consumer is probably one of the most abused consumers of any developed country around this world.

If we were to treat our consumers like they treat their consumers in Japan, we would probably have riots. But then we aren't Japanese.

No one has demonstrated better than the Japanese how well **protectionism** works.

Whenever people suggest using reciprocity, i.e.: treating the Japanese as they treat us, the free-traders warn of a depression in the order of magnitude of the 1930's which occurred right after the famous Smoot-Hawley tariff bill. All of these free traders (not fair traders) and liberal thinkers tell us if we do anything at all to disrupt our trade with Japan or make demands on them to open their markets many terrible things will happen. Today, this message is being spread, promoted and pushed very hard by Japan and their 'hirelings.' They are paid high fees to ensure that the Japanese message gets across and ours doesn't.

Let's examine how protectionism works so well in Japan, even though they don't admit they have protectionism.

Protectionism works in Japan partially because it is a saving culture, not a consuming one. It is a highly nationalistic one where buying Japanese is part of the ingrained culture.

Even though you may have heard these stories many times before, I feel they need to be repeated so we can examine the problem and possible solutions.

Before doing that, I would like to put to rest a myth which has been promoted by the do gooders in America and the Japanese 'hirelings.' The myth is that even if the Japanese did open their markets, our trade imbalance with Japan of about $50 billion per year would be changed very little. They point out the Japanese market is not as large as ours. They also make statements that our products are not very good and the Japanese wouldn't want them anyway. Fortunately, the arguments supporting that myth are quite false but they have rarely been refuted in the media.

Japan is really a very large market if the people were permitted to have the products to buy at a fair price. After all, ordinary beef at $20 to $25 a pound is a little too rich for most people. I'm sure if we had to pay that price in America, consumers wouldn't buy much either. There are many fine American products which those of us who had good success in Japan know the Japanese are anxious to buy.

In my experience the Japanese still bought American products even when they went through the complex Japanese distribution system and they had to pay the high duties and distribution costs which caused the products to cost several times what they cost in America.

We are all familiar with the high price of cars in Japan, especially imported cars, electronic gear, etc. The Japanese find it's often much cheaper to buy Japanese goods in America or Hong Kong instead of Japan.

Probably the single most important thing is a fact that the free traders and Japanese hirelings try to overlook. While opening the Japanese market will probably only increase our exports by

5, 10, or 15 billion dollars that is only part of the story. That is not the important point. The important point is that in allowing them to protect their markets and charge the high prices to their consumers and businesses and keep our products out, they don't have to face competition. If we could compete with them in Japan so they cannot build up these war chests to attack or subsidize other markets then you would find their products would become more expensive. Then we would be better able to compete with them in the rest of the world. That is where the real gain in our exports would take place.

Can you just imagine that if we prohibited all imports of beef to America and our government set the price at $20 a pound what a war chest we could set up to attack the rest of the world at cheap prices. I know you are going to say that would lead to illegal dumping. But the Japanese have developed a solution for that also which we could copy. You just don't sell the same model or item for export that you sell in your home market. They have been doing that with automobiles for years.

The fact that new products can be developed and sold in Japan for years with absolute protection from competition gives a new industry a great advantage. They only gradually open the market bit by bit after that company is very strong.

The Japanese have learned how to play the GATT (General Agreement on Tariffs and Trade) game better than any other country. They use the GATT rules very skillfully. If the GATT rules don't quite cover the situation, they bend them to fit. When you see some of their barriers, you are never quite sure which GATT article was being applied but they state it was according to GATT.

One of the GATT rules (XIII) implies that as long as you require all products sold in your country to comply with a given set of specifications it is all right. The Japanese set up safety specifications and require local testing and highly restrictive approval systems—in principle there is equality for all competing products of any given type, but in reality locally manufactured products have a distinct advantage.

By using GATT articles over the years, they have been able to keep out most products. First, it was Article XII, Balance of payments, then came Article XIII, Import Restrictions, then Article XIX, Emergency Action to restrict imports, then wonderful Article XX, General exceptions. And the catch all Article XXI, National Security. For example, the Japanese keep rice out on the grounds of food security. If we applied those same articles, we could make similar headway on solving our balance of trade problems.

One of their most effective rules to keep out imports is to require that the product be inspected in Japan and approved or returned to the overseas shipper. They used this on aluminum ball bats (until we forced a change), pressure vessels, automobiles, etc. I once lightheartedly suggested to the Japanese Consul General that we should inspect all Japanese cars after they arrived in America instead of letting them inspect and certify them before they left in Japan. He responded that would be very expensive and time consuming. I told him that would be no problem as we had a lot of unemployed auto workers whom the union would probably make available to inspect the Japanese imports.

Probably the most effective and widely used method of keeping products out of Japan is specifications. Not only does the government set specifications but also local trade organizations have specifications. These specifications are used in ways most people would never dream of.

I couldn't help but chuckle when we were advised that one specification was that **the product had to be manufactured in Japan** to be used by an organization. Now that's a good no nonsense way to keep imported products out of your country.

The aluminum baseball bat issue.—this wasn't significant in itself due to the small amount of business involved—illustrates very well many of the Japanese techniques for keeping products out of their country.

I had worked closely on this matter with Herb Cochran, American Consulate General in Tokyo. Herb had investigated this matter very carefully. It seems that some years ago there was an accident with an aluminum bat in Japan. As a consequence all imports of aluminum bats were banned. Only bats which had the Japanese safety seal could be used in Japan by their baseball league.

Herb worked to solve this problem with Howard Bruns of the Sporting Good Manufacturers of America and Mr. Fukada of the Japanese baseball league (JSBB) to get American bats approved. Mr. Fukada advised, "We, the JSBB **cannot approve articles made outside the country."**

A further investigation by Herb Cochran determined that the **accident was caused by a Japanese made bat.** For some unknown reason after this accident with a **Japanese** bat, the Japanese banned the import of all **American made bats.** Now this is real logic. If we have an **accident with an American car, we ban all Japanese cars.**

The reason Herb and all of us worked so long on this project was not just for bats. This issue of safety inspection applies to a **broad range** of products. That is why we filed an action with GATT. The Japanese also knew this was not just a bat issue but the GATT claim could cover many items.

So the Japanese finally agreed we could test bats in America before we shipped. Other **barriers** in the Japanese distribution system however held up sales.

A few other examples of Japanese protectionism:

Cigarettes
- For many years, there was no advertising of foreign cigarettes and they could only be sold in 10 percent of the retail outlets in the country. This was later improved **after much pressure.** They reduced the duty on tobacco

products from 90% to 35% and they think that is **very low.** I wonder if we put a 35% duty on Japanese cars if they would think that was **very low.**

Rice
- You know you are not dealing on a level playing field when you get the Japanese government reaction after the U.S. Rice Miller's Association filed a petition to impose retaliatory measures if Japan failed to open its rice market.

The Japanese Agriculture Minister said, "Japan's trade system on food is permitted under GATT."
- All rice imports are prohibited by the government so imported rice does not compete with local farmers. If we had a similar prohibition on automobiles they would scream. One justification for the prohibition on rice imports is that they are protecting the symbol of their ancient agrarian heritage. To further justify this action they have many other excuses like foreign rice is bad, or they must have "food security." They have given all kinds of such excuses and as long as we let them get away with it they will.

Later in 1991, the Japanese threatened to arrest Americans for just **displaying** rice at an American exhibition in Japan. I wonder what would happen if we prohibited the display of cars imported from Japan?

Citrus fruits—Many times when I have been in Japan, I read in the papers that another shipment of citrus fruits from America has been held up at the docks on some technicality.

We experienced the same thing with many of our products over the years.

When we shipped to Japan lacquer finishes or oil conditioners for our equipment, it would be stopped at the docks. They would then demand the formula for the product. We would send them a list of all the contents. They would not accept that.

They wanted the precise proportions of each ingredient and any special process the product had been through. We would finally give them that information very reluctantly. Weeks would pass and finally the product would be released. About the same time, very strangely, an identical Japanese product would come on the market. We always knew there was a great cooperation between business and government but that looked like **collusion** to us. On the other hand, maybe the manufacturer had not received our formula but had only been given time to analyze the product. We don't know what they did. We only know the result.

We were not allowed to include in our tool kits tape measures that were calibrated in both inches and metric. Only metric could be on the tape.

They have a thousand devices to keep your products out of Japan and they are probably developing new ones every day.

So when the Japanese put out a news story that they have opened their market, take it with a grain of salt. You have only passed the first barrier.

All of the details of this story are in the Congressional Committee Hearing Records. I testified before Senator Heinz together with the beef and electronics representatives about our problems with Japanese trade barriers.

It was interesting to note that in the hearing room the audience included only a Japanese T.V. crew and a number of other people who were apparently lobbyists for Japan.

The following week, we saw our pictures and an article on the hearing in Japanese newspapers. You can see the Japanese leave no stone unturned when it comes to trying to keep their barriers in place and the American market open.

The Japanese have proven protectionism does work. There would be no great consequences to the world if we also take steps to protect our markets as they have protected theirs. It will also open up the possibility to have some real good and meaningful trade reform for the world.

Always remember, if a trade war would develop, Japan would lose its $50 billion/year trade surplus with the U.S.A. We would lose very little.

In my many years of working with the Japanese, I have found that they may not always be nice but they are much too smart to lose the $50 billion per year.

We have had some recent experiences in this area when President Reagan put various restrictions on Toshiba for illegally exporting American Technology to the U.S.S.R. There was a lot of noise from Japan but no retaliation against America. The 100% tariff on the Toshiba products of computers, T.V.s, drills, etc., had very little negative effect on the American consumer or our relations with Japan. The large retail chains said they had many other sources for these products from other countries. This refutes another myth which is promoted by other people who are not our friends.

Another most interesting trade barrier in Japan is the list of industries where foreigners are not allowed to participate. A meeting was held at the Japan Society in New York where the honored guest was Mr. Toyoo Gyoten, Deputy Director General of the Ministry of Finance. Mr. Gyoten's mission was to explain to U.S. businessmen how Japan had liberalized the policy on foreign investment.

During the question and answer period, the Vice President of the Bendix Corporation indicated it was very difficult to do anything in the aviation field. Mr. Gyoten advised that was because aviation comes under national defense and investment is not permitted. Gyoten was advised that Mitsubishi had an aircraft plant in Texas. This then caused Gyoten to list all the industries we can't invest in such as media, agriculture, etc., etc. I commented that we had been invited to hear how open Japan was, but got a bigger list of things we couldn't invest in. I suggested if we had similar regulations in America they would not be allowed to invest in the automobile industry. His American lawyer became very upset that I should make such a statement. He apparently felt it was very embarrassing to this high official. Since I felt they probably needed more explanation of my statement about the auto industry, I commented that Mr. Gyoten said we cannot invest in their defense industry. If we had a similar rule, Japan couldn't invest in the auto industry. Their American lawyer shouted, "Gibberish." I went on to say in 1940 and 1941, I worked at the Ford Motor Company. At the Highland Park plant where I worked, we produced MI tanks. At the other Ford plant at Willow Run, we were turning out B-24 Bombers at a tremendous rate and I certainly thought that was a part of our defense industry. This prompted a few more unkind remarks by the American lawyer.

The next morning on the front page of the *Journal of Commerce* was the headline on an article, "AMF Aid Challenges Japan on Discrimination." As it turned out, Mr. Gyoten's statement of how open they were ended up being how closed Japan was.

Another very interesting way to keep America out of their market is stealing the technology of our U.S. patents by not granting a patent in Japan. This will be discussed in detail in a later chapter.

In my many discussions with the Japanese on their protectionist policies, I have had some success calling attention to their policies in a lighthearted manner. This is most difficult as the Japanese are not very big on humor. But they do understand English very well. They are very much aware of their tactics to keep products out of Japan but they get very upset if you address the subject directly. Hence, the attempt at humor or a story to illustrate the point.

The most effective approaches are to give them a backhanded compliment on their policies. In effect, we tell them it's a great idea and we should copy **their** policy exactly. If they have such a policy it must be good and very correct.

A few examples of their trade barriers and my suggestions to them.

Beef
- Some years ago, I told Ambassador Asao's staff (when I was complaining about this protectionism) that I saw two bumper stickers in the Midwest which read, "A Cow for A Car" and "A Ton of Beef for a Toyota." I told them it sounded like a very fair trade off, but they didn't like the idea.

Cigarettes
- Japan's restrictions on U.S.A. cigarettes. For years it restricted all advertising on imported cigarettes but allowed full advertising on local cigarettes. That was bad but the real problem was imported cigarettes could only be sold in 10% of the outlets and I can assure you they were not the best outlets.
- I suggested to Mr. Hirai at Jetro in New York that the Japanese had a great idea—sell in only 10% of the outlets. Would he object if we let them sell Japanese cars in only 10% of our states—and I suggested Utah, New Mexico, Louisiana, Rhode Island and Michigan. He thought that was a very bad idea of mine but he still felt limiting our sales in Japan was a good idea.

Rice
- All rice imported to Japan is controlled by the government. They really have a virtual ban on imports but sometimes they buy a little if local production is not adequate. They then price the imported rice so it doesn't compete with local farmers. I suggested to a Japanese official that again that was a good idea.

Why didn't we in the U.S.A. have our government buy all the Japanese VCRs and then set a price so they didn't hurt our local industry (if we had one). Even though our government wouldn't really protect our local industry as Japan does, I was sure the massive bureaucracy in Washington would probably double or triple the domestic U.S. sales price. The Japanese official thought that was a very bad idea.

Since it is quite clear that they have no intention of really opening their markets, reciprocity is probably the only solution. As far back as 1982 when Senator Heinz was conducting congressional hearings, he made it perfectly clear that was the only workable solution. Most of the business people I knew agreed. But nothing really happened with our trade negotiators along this line for years. I was very pleased to hear in May 1991, that we are threatening to do just that with regard to construction contracts. I just hope it's not an idle threat as we have seen so many times in the past. And the Japanese know we are weak and probably won't carry it out.

As long as that weak attitude prevails in Washington, I am afraid we will not get much satisfaction on our trade problems. Japanese businessmen I have known wonder why we let them get away with this. They feel we are very dumb. But they are not going to complain since it is great for their companies.

Over the years, I have come to realize our trade negotiators are more interested in keeping the Japanese happy and less interested in our unemployed, poor and homeless. This state of affairs is probably the direct result of their incompetence or lack of courage.

In all fairness, I probably shouldn't criticize our negotiators so severely when they get out-negotiated, they just don't have the experience and often their hands are tied. Most are in the job only a few years and it takes them the first few years to learn what they are to do. They may be famous lawyers, officials, etc., but they are just amateurs up against the skilled Japanese negotiators who have been doing the same thing for years and who have "Japan, Inc." behind them.

On the other hand, if we would follow the Japanese practice on restricting imports, we know it would have a very favorable effect on American industry.

There is the famous case of Harley-Davidson motorcycles. A few years ago, Harley, the only remaining American manufacturer of motorcycles, was in deep trouble from Japanese imports. President Reagan approved imposing a 45% duty on all imported motorcycles over 700 CC. This action gave Harley the time and breathing room to improve their quality, develop their markets and get their costs under control. A few years later, Harley-Davidson was doing so well they asked the U.S. government to **remove** the **high duty.**

With this temporary help, Harley-Davidson has done so well it now has over 60% of the American market. More than all the Japanese manufacturers combined.

Not only have they recaptured the American market but their exports have soared. They were doing a few million dollars a year in exports when they were a part of AMF and now I understand their exports are over $100 million. Japan is now one of their major export markets. You should read the book *Well Made in America* by Peter Reid.

We should copy this Japanese approach to protectionism for many of our other industries. This is reciprocity in action. Playing hardball with the Japanese has good effects, not bad effects.

This approach can also help out the poor Japanese consumers who are suffering almost as much due to the Japanese trade barriers as we are. They are restricted from buying fine imported products at fair prices. Part of our goal should be to try and help the Japanese consumer.

We are not mad at the Japanese people anymore than we were mad at the Iraqi people during the Desert Storm. It is only the leaders we have the problem with and this seems to apply equally in both cases. ☐

Chapter 6:

PATIENCE, PATIENCE IS REALLY DELAY, DELAY

STARTING SOME THIRTY years ago, after the Japanese had recovered from the terrible war they started in the 1930's in China and with America in 1941, they set up some new strategies.

They very carefully painted a picture to the world that they were a poor, kind, undeveloped nation that needed all sorts of help. They kept saying we should be very patient and not complain about their closed markets as their companies were so weak. We should all help them by opening our markets so they could earn hard currency. At the time, there was some small amount of truth to some of those statements, but we didn't realize it was part of a plan. The story goes that their quality was so poor that at one time they produced some product in a small town called USA and they marked the products "Made in USA." Their autos were so bad that in Japan and Southeast Asia the word was never keep a Japanese car more than three years as it starts to fall apart.

I kept hearing the Japanese tell me as late as the late 1970's that we should be very patient as they were so undeveloped. They did a wonderful job of convincing the world that we had to help that poor country. It was possible to keep up that facade when you looked at the ordinary consumer in Japan who had to pay very high prices for almost anything they bought due to a lack of competition from world products and the inefficient distribution system.

If you looked at the terrible housing conditions, the lack of sewers, roads, etc., you could be convinced it was like a poor developing nation. Even today they have not made much progress to help the people. The money is all channeled to economically dominate the world. But they are no longer a developing nation.

Of late, we have observed them changing their spots very quickly. Suddenly, they are the greatest, arrogant, pushy, condescending, etc. They tell us if they don't buy our treasury securities our country will go bankrupt. The famous Ishihara (of *Japan Can Say No*) says we are at their mercy. If they won't sell us chips, our U.S. military couldn't function—and on and on it goes.

This all plays very well with the media who like to have negative stories about America.

The Japanese and their hirelings have done a particularly good job of brainwashing the young people of America into feeling that only the Japanese can make superior products.

Most of the world doesn't seem to realize this long term Japanese trade strategy. It was done so quietly at first and it was done with patience, patience, patience. And then they delay, delay, delay any actions on complaints.

If you review the U.S./Japan trade problems, you will note that they never take any meaningful action until they are put under intense pressure. This usually requires you to embarrass them publicly. Then a little give by the Japanese. My own experience has been the same.

With their excellent public relations campaign they usually do nothing to react to normal complaints. They just keep putting out news stories like they did in 1990, "Japanese Pledge Lower Barriers to Trade With U.S." or "U.S., Japan to Discuss Citrus Policy" or "Japan Yields to U.S. on Chips" or "Japan Reduces Duties on 50 Items." But nothing really happens. The trade deficit keeps growing. If not directly with Japan then by means of their offshore plants. The stories from Tokyo really haven't changed for 30 years. It's just that they are getting better at fooling us.

If you have followed this carefully, as I have for some 30 years, you should then pick up a copy of *National Trade Estimate On*

Foreign Trade Barriers put out by the Office of the U.S. Trade Representative. You can read through page after page after page of the trade barriers that still exist. If you had believed all those headlines and the stories from Tokyo, you would have thought they had all been solved.

Over the years, I have learned one simple truth on how to deal with Japan on these matters. The only way we have been able to make any reasonable progress on any issue is to be very firm if not tough and, usually, this also requires you to embarrass them publicly. Just look at the positive results we got in three cases:

1) when Congress embarrassed them over the Desert Storm contributions,
2) when IBM filed an action for stealing IBM secrets. (The Japanese called the settlement a "National Disgrace"), and
3) when Toshiba sold our secrets to the U.S.S.R. and we put 100% duties on Toshiba products.

Except for these few cases, however we have no victories with Japan. If you really want to get the Japanese attention, you have to do things like France and Italy who restrict Japanese car imports to 3% of the market. Or the famous action by France when it decided that the only port of entry of VCR's to France was the tiny city of Poitiers in western France. I understand they only had a couple of customs agents in Poitiers and the VCR's piled up in warehouses. The French had really only copied a variation of Japan tactics. The immediate Japanese complaint was to claim **a violation of GATT rules.**

Another way to head off criticism is to pull a publicity stunt. A few years ago, Prime Minister Nakasone undertook what I call his "great publicity stunt." All Japanese consumers should buy $100 worth of American goods. He knew it wouldn't amount to a hill of beans. He knew that very few Japanese took such public pronouncements seriously. It was only done for foreign consumption. He also knew that because of the markup along the Japanese distribution system a $100 sale is really about $20 worth of imported American goods.

To really get something done, he should have turned to "administrative guidance" and had MITI issue the word that Japanese car companies should put American tires, filters, and spark plugs, etc. on all cars going to the U.S. That would have done some good.

What further complicates solving our trade differences are the articles and speeches advocating restraint and peace with Japan by such people as Cyrus Vance and William Gleysteen, Chairman and President of the Japan Society, respectively. You see these people, apparently in good conscience, but probably with a conflict of interest due to their association with the Japan Society, making all kinds of unfortunate statements. They tell us we desperately need Japan for National Security reasons. They tell us to stop criticizing Japan, to blunt our anti-Japanese rhetoric. They warn us about the slippery slope of protectionism. The Japanese have found that protectionism for their market is not a slippery slope. In fact, it is a slope paved with gold as they practice it with perfection.

These types of people warn us we have to put our own house in order as we are really a mess. But all such Japanese friends seem to be very quiet when Japan issues stern warnings if the U.S. applies restrictions on Japan similar to those Japan places on the U.S. in their financial markets. The Japanese threaten indirectly to stop buying our bonds, and creating a very harmful situation!! Therefore, we must have patience, patience, patience in dealing with Japan.

We hear the comments of Mr. Ohtsuka, a former Deputy Consul General in New York criticizing Senator Heinz for his very realistic, fair appraisal and solutions to the U.S./Japan trade problems. Mr. Ohtsuka seems to imply we should not criticize Japan, the problem is all our fault.

It is quite clear that patience will not solve our problems with Japan as our trade deficit with Japan has increased significantly in the last decade.

You can see we will not have a solution from our government and we must resort to other means which will be discussed later. Hopefully, these other means should end this constant government to government badgering and constant criticism of businesses by the lobbyists for trying to solve this problem. □

Chapter 7:

HOW TO CAPTURE MARKETS THE JAPANESE WAY

ONE OF THE first lessons I learned at West Point is to fight your battles off shore. By the time the enemy has a beachhead on your land, it is probably too late. When I became involved in the business world, I realized that statement was even more true.

The Japanese have a simple plan for gaining world dominance in any particular field.

- **Step 1:** Set up barriers, tariff and non-tariff, so others can't sell into their markets and compete. This gives local industries time to develop the know-how, quality and strength needed to start competing in world markets. (It's too bad if, for a while, domestic consumers pay sky-high prices for shoddy goods).
- **Step 2:** Make the initial push into smaller markets where you won't be noticed and markets close to home.
- **Step 3:** Chase all indigenous competition out with predatory pricing. Even if it means selling at a loss, Japanese companies undercut their competition until everyone else is out of business. The Japanese companies would also be out of business if they weren't receiving such favorable treatment from their government and banks and if their own domestic consumers weren't still buying their goods at such high prices because there is little competition back home.
- **Step 4:** Once all competitors are gone, raise the prices and start banking the profits and getting ready to attack the next country or market.

I have seen this happen many times, but let me give you a specific example. In 1978, the three electric divisions of our company were selling about $25,000 per year into Southeast Asia (Singapore, Taiwan, Malaysia, etc.). We hired one salesman in Singapore and later a second one to work out of Hong Kong to cover the areas. In two years, we were taking orders at the rate of $1 million a month. In fact, our U.S. factories could not fill the orders in a timely manner.

In discussing the success with our sales people, they confirmed again our understanding of Japanese strategy. Our new customers had told our salesmen if they could offer a product comparable to the Japanese product they were currently buying at a price no more than 10% above the Japanese, they would give us at least 10% of the business.

The customers confirmed to our people that they needed us very badly, as they knew once the Japanese had no competition the prices would just keep going up until they in turn were run out of business.

You will keep seeing this over and over—it doesn't matter to Japan if they lose money or make only a small amount on a new product in the U.S.A.—such as Lexus or Infiniti and sell it for $30,000 or $40,000 against the BMW, Mercedes, etc., that sell for twice as much—because at some time in the future as they control enough of the market they can raise their prices.

Some people call this predatory pricing. To us who have dealt with them over the years, this is SOP—Standard Operating Procedure for the Japanese. While this Japanese strategy has been known by many people for years, very few have done anything about it.

Most American companies are quite satisfied to just sell to the American market as long as the business makes a reasonable profit. What the people don't understand is what is going on in the world markets. Once a company overseas makes a similar product and has developed a large market in many countries it is quite easy for them to attack the American market. They probably have lower labor costs and lower overall costs due to economies of scale. Since they have a large world market they can price their product very aggressively to attack the American market. Then you see the American company in financial trouble in a few years. At this point we see a new Step #5 in this Japanese strategy.

- **Step 5:** The Japanese offer to buy this beaten American company. They present themselves as the Great Savior. The Governor of the state where the plant is located thanks the Japanese for saving the company and all those jobs. The media covers the story on the front page with pictures of a smiling Governor and many smiling Japanese, who know how well their strategy is working. And, instead of people being angry with them they are grateful.

Soon the same will happen to another American company that failed to fight its battles overseas. There is probably no one who reads this book who hasn't seen this happen to a company near them.

The pace is picking up as America becomes more and more a colony of Japan. This doesn't just happen in industry, but also in agriculture, entertainment and universities as the Japanese become the Great Savior.

The sad part of this story is that the companies never realized how they let themselves be put into that position of weakness.

But the Japanese don't just stop at capturing markets by those nice means. They also use other tactics. These tactics are really quite disgusting. For example: "Nippon Steel Settles Patent Suit." It seems Allegheny Ludlum, a specialty steel manufacturer, patented a process for grain oriented silicon electrical steel in 1974. In 1984, Allegheny accused Nippon Steel of using the patent without compensation or permission. After many attempts to settle this misuse of a patent, which Nippon kept rejecting, they finally settled in 1991 for a few million dollars.

This is a great way to capture a market. You, in effect, use the patent, develop a major world market and then after many years make a small settlement. You can easily afford the settlement once you are so strong and profitable. It's not nice but it works.

Then we see another way for a Japanese company to capture world markets with the help of the U.S. Government. Some years ago when the Russians were building the large pipeline from the U.S.S.R. to Western Europe, the U.S. Government became very upset with the U.S.S.R. over Afghanistan. The U.S. banned all American companies from supplying equipment to build the pipeline. Caterpillar, who made the world's best pipe laying machinery, was forbidden to ship any more products. Komatsu of Japan (Caterpillar's main competitor) took over all the business and became an even stronger company.

Then we later see the same old story repeated. Governor Lamar Alexander of Tennessee congratulated Komatsu's Mr. Nogawa for opening a plant in Chattanooga to make equipment competitive to Caterpillar. They note that Caterpillar lost money in 1983 and 1984 due to the loss of its export markets to Komatsu. If you look into the story of the plant a little deeper you note that Komatsu's plant will be a "screwdriver" plant. Just assembling imported Japanese components. Because of this many more Americans lose good jobs.

Probably the greatest way to capture a key world market goes back to the area of patents. I recall the famous or infamous story of how the Japanese refused to grant a patent in Japan for the famous Kilby patent of Texas Instruments. This is the key patent for virtually all integrated circuits. It is estimated that the Japanese market for integrated circuits is about $17 billion per year. Apparently, most use this patented information. Texas Instrument was granted the U.S. patent in 1964. It applied for the patent in Japan in 1960. The Japanese took 29 years to grant this key basic patent on chips. In the meantime, using what some people might consider stolen technology, they built their integrated circuit industry to be the largest in the world. **(But All is Fair in Love, War and Business).**

A Japanese financial newspaper estimates that if standard royalties are paid by Japanese companies, they will have to pay Texas Instruments about $500 to $700 million a year.

But what about the past? Our government should take action against Japan not only to recover the $10 to $15 billion dollars due to Texas Instruments for past royalties plus interest but also for triple damages for doing so much damage to American industries.

In 1990, 11 of the 20 largest banks in the world were Japanese. The largest American bank, Citicorp was 20th.

This great success of the Japanese banks is probably due more to the restrictions Japan has on financial services and trade, than on their ability.

This is one more example of Japan's efforts toward economic domination of the world. But, **All is Fair in Love, War and Business.**

You must realize that when you deal with Japan, they don't play fair. That is just one more reason why this book is dedicated to the unemployed, the minorities, the poor and our future graduates who may never find a good job in America unless we act strongly. □

Chapter 8:

HOW TO COMPROMISE PEOPLE, COMPANIES, AND GOVERNMENTS

WHEN YOU SAY something critical about the Japanese, that is "Japan Bashing." When they say something critical about America "that's because we deserve it." This just gives you some idea of how effectively they have compromised the media and many influential people in the U.S.A. You do have to congratulate them on such an effective campaign.

When I testified before a Congressional committee, the only people in attendance were Japanese reporters and camera crews and Americans who worked as lobbyists for Japanese companies.

In the last two decades, the Japanese have spent hundreds of millions of dollars to influence American legislation, both federally and at the state level. (See Choate's *Agents of Influence*)

The Japanese have just about written our trade laws, manufacturing, investment and banking rules over the past two decades. They have conducted such an effective propaganda campaign in the United States that we now feel we cannot produce goods as inexpensively and as well as the Japanese. They make sure our government officials create policies that they approve. They compromise educators. They compromise the Media.

Agents of Influence by Pat Choate gets to the heart of the problem. Choate's book should be required reading of every government official, elected or appointed, and most Americans so that they all fully understand how they have been manipulated by Japan.

Unfortunately, some of these people will use it as a guide as to how they should butter up the Japanese by their actions in the government so they can be hired by the Japanese when they leave government service.

One of the most important and little known facts is related in Choate's book in Chapter 12, why Japan's most ambitious propaganda campaign is aimed at American educators and the U.S. Media. "How the Media Broadcasts Japans Own Propaganda." How the Japanese are reshaping American education. Why the Japanese give free trips to Japan for elementary and secondary teachers in effect to brainwash them to say the things about Japan that the Japanese want said. Many of us have seen this in business but to do this to innocent elementary education teachers is going pretty far. We all know how Hitler worked on the youth through their teachers to get his message across with sad eventual results to the world.

The interesting thing about being compromised is that many people don't realize they have been compromised. This has been one area where the Japanese have shown their greatest skill.

It takes many forms and usually starts out quite innocently. I first noticed it in Japan in 1948. My wife would mention to me that wives of other military personnel who were acquaintances of ours, would show their beautiful pearls or other jewelry that were gifts to their husbands from the Japanese. She was quite curious why I was never given any gifts!

Later, when we were setting up a manufacturing plant in Japan in the late 1960's, our U.S. plant manager would mention how on many nights when he or members of his staff when back to the hotel they would find cameras, HiFis, and so forth in their rooms as gifts from potential suppliers. He would bring the gifts back to the factory the following day and return them to the supplier. Then you see the former U.S. governmental official who has worked very closely with the Japanese. When he or she leaves the government you notice they show up in some very fine job with that Japanese company. Then we see the next type—the government official, congressman, who returns to his or her old law firm and lobbies for Japanese companies.

A high Japanese official was asked if that could ever happen in Japan. His answer was a firm NO!! If it ever did, that person would be ostracized from society. He could not have any effect on the government's decision.

We did, however, have a case that was very close when former Prime Minister Tanaka was tried for allegedly accepting a bribe from Lockheed to help them get an order from a commercial Japanese airline. It has been pointed out however that he was influencing a company, not the government. They would look upon anyone who would consider such lobbying a traitor.

On May 2, 1982, the *Detroit News* did an in-depth article titled "Japan Lobby: Made in USA" which lists many former key government officials who lobby for Japan—"the largest and best financed army of lobbyists in Washington marches under the flag of the Land of the Rising Sun."

The story it relates is quite unbelievable. The sad part is that their main job is to influence the legislation and policy of the United States to stop the U.S. Government from taking any positive action to reduce the trade deficit with Japan. The article points out that a Ms. Dudeck was co-author of a U.S. International Trade Commission Report in 1980. Her report concluded that Japanese auto imports were not hurting our U.S. auto industry. That would normally only have been thought of as a bad report if Ms. Dudeck hadn't taken a job a few months later as a very high official in Honda's Washington office.

At that time, our trade deficit with Japan was only about $25 billion. Now that Japan has strengthened its efforts to influence American government, you can understand why our trade deficit has risen to over $50 billion.

An accompanying article in the *Detroit News* the same day also shows the shocking infiltration of our media by the Japanese. You soon realize that many of our news articles may have been influenced by the Japanese as Choate also points out.

I am sure that none of the famous people listed consider themselves compromised, they are just doing a job for which they are paid very well.

We saw the same story all over again in the *New York Times* on December 10, 1989. Nothing had really changed. Only the date on the article and a new list of lobbyists. The story is the same only there are many more names of former government officials working for the Japanese. Now we hear how they are even trying to infiltrate our universities with large grants. Everyone says this is all arms length and no one is being influenced. If you really believe that, you also like to get paid in $3 bills or you still believe in the tooth fairy.

I have suggested to some congressmen that they should enact a bill which would prohibit any former government official, appointed or elected, from working for a foreign entity for 10 years after leaving the government.

Senator Heinz was a leader in understanding this problem and was actively working to solve it before his untimely death. Now there are many other people compromised in many different ways. It will be almost impossible to get such a bill passed as congressmen and administration officials will have to take a position. If they favor the bill that means they will lose their opportunity to become a highly paid Japanese lobbyist.

There was an excellent investigative article in the *Wall Street Journal* on February, 23, 1990, with the sub-title "Many American (Trade) Negotiators once worked for Japanese and May Again in Future." Even our U.S. Trade Representative, Carla Hills, once briefly advised Matsushita Electric Company on anti-dumping.

Her husband, Roderick Hills, practices law with the head of Nissan's lobbying firm. The Hills are apparently good friends of C. Itoh's Washington Representative.

In fact, it seems that some former officials in the U.S. Trade Representative office ended up working for or advising the Japanese in one way or another. They are all doing much better than our unemployed auto workers.

Once you recognize all this Japanese power in Washington, it is easier to understand how the Japanese got our officials in Washington to **reclassify** Japanese **pickup trucks** to cars, to avoid the 25% import duty. Then, as soon as they crossed our boarder, they get them **reclassified** to trucks, so they wouldn't have to meet the more stringent controls on cars regarding pollution, safety, and so forth.

You wonder how the people who did this or those who permitted it to happen can sleep at night. But **All is Fair in Love, War and Business.** It's only the poor and middle income Americans who have to pay the price.

You cannot help but be bothered by the Japanese penetration into our education system and our universities.

- The heavy financing of studies at our universities. The $10 million agreement with the Massachusetts Institute of Technology to teach Japanese scientists how to replicate a laboratory for research areas involving computer science.
- The purchase of some of our colleges. I often find that when I give speeches at colleges they are not happy with my position on Japan as it is contrary to their efforts to get Japanese funds.

As I mentioned earlier, the Japanese have done an excellent job gaining the support of our local officials. If an American company opens up a new factory or office in a state it's hardly noticed. But when the Japanese do it a major media event is promoted. The governor, mayor, and other officials all appear. Often times the new factory is a result of a local firm having been run out of business by the unfair Japanese competition and, then, the Japanese Savior arrives to buy the company or factory.

Then we have the companies that have been compromised by the Japanese. These compromises take many forms.

First, we have the companies that sell or distribute a Japanese product in America. They all do their best to support their Japanese suppliers because it's their livelihood. They want to eat. They also want to try and avoid the inevitable outcome which has happened to the distributors of other Japanese products — Sony — Canon, etc. They were cut out and taken over by the Japanese once they got well established.

They also help spread the Japanese propaganda something like this, "My Japanese car dealership employs a lot of people and if you put restrictions on the import of Japanese cars, I will have to lay off many people."

They seem to have forgotten the hundreds of thousands of American workers that have lost their jobs because of the imported cars. I mentioned that one time when I was discussing the Japanese barriers on rice and meat with a Japanese government official. He said if they lower those barriers, Japanese farmers will be out of work. When I said how about the thousands of American auto workers that were put out of work by imported Japanese cars. His comment— oh, that's different. End of discussion. I guess it's the old story of "Whose ox is being gored."

Then there are the other U.S. companies who are compromised not because they want to — but they do business in Japan and, if they speak out against Japanese barriers or lobbying or if they offer any other criticism of the Japanese they will have problems. These will be silent sobering actions taken by the Japanese. Maybe you will find it difficult to hire Japanese employees. Maybe they will investigate you for something to disrupt your business. Maybe other Japanese customers will suddenly not want to buy from you. Maybe you will encounter more delays at customs, and so forth.

So companies like Coca Cola, IBM, Corning, DOW, Merrill Lynch, Chase Bank, must be very careful in their actions or statements. I don't blame those companies because they are quite helpless in many ways. I am still amazed that IBM had the courage to take the strong action it did against Hitachi regarding industrial espionage.

The first group which has been compromised are people in general. Probably a better word than "compromised" is "brainwashed." People have been fed so much very subtle Japanese propaganda from many sources that they don't even realize they have been brainwashed. At least not until they lose their job.

Every environmentalist among them should be shocked at the Japanese owned company being subsidized by the U.S. Government (that's U.S. taxpayers) and sold lumber (up to 4.5 billion board feet every 10 years) at below market prices. The finances are bad enough not to mention losing so much of this old forest to foreigners in the form of rough logs. This export of raw material provides very little employment. We should have a law like the Indonesians who prohibit the export of unprocessed logs.

The important point about the Japanese is not the large amounts of money paid to the lobbyists to compromise our government and others. The important point is the terrible results it will have on our lives and our children's lives for years to come.

We have had "Benedict Arnolds" around us since the Revolutionary War. The Japanese lobbyists are possibly the modern day "Benedict Arnolds." Let's just not let them destroy our country and our lives too much or too easily. □

Chapter 9:

THE JAPANESE LONG RANGE PLAN

I TRUST THAT by now you have begun to realize that the Japanese are not buying our bonds, buildings, land and companies because they like us. I am convinced this is only our introduction to a longer range plan, which if we let them succeed will be very bad for us and the world. Ishihara in the book *Japan That Can Say No* has hinted at this. This is probably the greatest threat our country has faced since World War II or the Great Depression.

As they begin to control more of our key industries, our media companies (such as MCA and Columbia Pictures), you will see how they control our strengths and our minds. As they seek world domination of autos, electronics, aircraft, etc., you will see how subjected we all become. Something like modern day slaves.

I see the Japanese plan for world economic domination following some of the same lines of their old Tanaka plan of the early 1900's. (Gen. Giichi Tanaka, who was Prime Minister of Japan from 1926-29 had advanced a plan to Emperor Hirohito regarding the domination of Manchuria and China that he believed would result in a hopeless war with the United States **unless** - Japan had control of the raw material and factories of Asia). The new plan is more economic and less militaristic. As I recall, the old Tanaka plan went something like this through it's various phases:

1) Build up the military
2) Capture China
3) Control Southeast Asia
4) Fight America
5) Dominate the world

My view of their new plan for world domination follows many similar phases. Some of these have been alluded to in earlier chapters:
1) Close Japanese markets (both manufacturers and service)
2) Build up manufacturing industries
3) Capture markets in Southeast Asia and raw material sources
4) Brainwash U.S. Government leaders, educators, media, etc.
5) Control U.S. Government actions on trade
6) Infiltrate every strategic U.S. industry
7) Capture U.S. markets
8) Build up huge cash supplies
9) Capture European markets
10) Control China market and raw material sources

The Japanese long range plan will never be revealed any more than their negotiators told our officials in Washington, on Sunday morning, December 7, 1941, that their planes had taken off to bomb Pearl Harbor while they were still negotiating.

Some people will say that, with comments like this, I am "Japan Bashing" when I am really only stating a fact. When you hear that comment from some westerner you at least know who has been compromised. You have to accept that the Japanese will keep repeating it regardless of what we say.

As I have observed the actions of the Japanese for many years, I am convinced that they feel the only way they can live down their defeat in World War II and their criminal acts all through Asia is to show the world they are in control, that they have an economic stranglehold on the world, that they are superior to other people in the world.

This has been evident in the speeches of Prime Minister Nakasone and of various other public officials which I have previously discussed.

A few years ago, Mr. Okuno, a Cabinet Minister, visited the national shrine honoring Japan's war dead and was quoted as saying, "Japan fought the war in order to secure its safety. ... The white race has turned Asia into a colony. Japan was by **no means the aggressor nation."**

Both China and Korea protested. But scarcely any notice was taken in the West. Forty-one right-wing members of the ruling Liberal Democratic Party had come out in support of Mr. Okuno and denounced criticism of Japan's role in the war.

As it was, Seisuke Okuno was obliged to resign from his Cabinet post as Director General of Japan's National Land Agency. But there has been no real apology, as far as I know.

You have seen this superior attitude in the Japanese edition of the book by Sony Chairman Morita and Shintaro Ishihara titled *The Japan That Can Say No.*

You see it in the frustration of some Japanese leaders when they say "If you put up trade barriers, we are going to turn to the Communists"—that was a good line a few years ago, but it is a little more difficult now to find communist countries with any power or money to buy from them.

You see this attitude in business. When a major U.S. magazine was running a special 50th anniversary edition of the outbreak of World War II, a strange thing happened. Prior to the publication of this series, the Japanese had saturated the magazine with their ads—Acura, Infiniti, Mitsubishi, Mazda, etc.—and had many multi-page ads.

When the series went into publication, however there were **no** ads for their cars at all. Coincidence or planned? They just can't stand **public** embarrassment and they take strong actions to show it. Just wait until some producer at Columbia Pictures (now owned by Sony) tries to do a negative picture on Japan—you will never hear about it—but you can be sure Sony will never let the picture be made. But it will be denied quietly. They may decide there are more appropriate pictures to invest their money in or some other excuse.

But if the director or producer is smart, he will do a movie on the superiority of Japanese products, or inferior American labor, or weak U.S. management, and he will be rewarded. The Japanese will have made one more step in the brainwashing of America. Then you will see how effectively they have executed their long range domination plan. Nothing is left to chance.

In the newspapers and on TV you hear and see these articles saying the Japanese economy is in big trouble. It is reported that exports are dropping, the yen is sinking, wages are up, profits down, etc., so you will feel sorry for that poor country. The implication is maybe we should help them out.

Senator Gephardt had a good idea during his presidential campaign with his tough talk on trade. But he was no match for all the powerful lobbyists and other powerful Japanese hirelings. He was probably defeated by the Japanese on that part of his program but most likely didn't realize it.

The Japanese effort to dominate key industries, such as Integrated Circuits and Chips, is another part of their key strategy to dominate the world and hold us all hostage. You may think the Iran hostage situation was bad, but you haven't seen anything yet. However you will hardly notice it is happening as it gradually creeps up on you. You must always remember you are dealing with some very smart long range planners. I'm sure the radio, car, TV, chip and computer manufacturers didn't realize at first what was happening until they were in very deep trouble or out of business.

I think the greatest success the Japanese have had in implementing their plan of world domination has been the great, but I hope innocent, support by well meaning government officials and the media. Week after week we hear and read these stories of how Japan is cutting exports to the USA.

In November 1986 they announced big cuts in textile and machine tool exports to the USA. In 1987, they announced they were cutting tariffs on aluminum imports. The stories go on and on almost daily. It is still happening in 1991.

What is probably happening to these government and media people is what happened to the media in New York in January 1990, when a young lady had a big party to announce she had won a $30 million lottery prize. There were big stories in all the media, but they had been conned! She had made it all up.

The same is true with most of these stories. The media has published the statements of the Japanese government or it hirelings but rarely does anyone follow up to see what really happens. We have all been conned.

It is my impression that they keep putting out these stories to disarm us. For example, about once a year we read a big story "Japanese trade surplus narrows" or words to that effect. That was probably true for a month, but then you see the year end story—very low key—that there is a big increase in the trade deficit with Japan. This goes on year after year.

If they want to completely ban a product from Japan they just do it. They even complain when some group such as the U.S. rice producers demand that Japan open its markets. They have many reasons not to agree. It's all right to ban under GATT Rules, the Japanese farmers are upset, the Japanese don't mind paying five to six times as much more for Japanese rice than American rice, and so forth.

As I keep saying, the Japanese feel **"all is fair in love, war and business."** As long as it advances the long range plan of world economic domination! With friends like this, who needs enemies!!

I do not feel we should be too concerned when the Japanese buy up land or buildings in America. Always remember that they can't take them home. If they raise the rent too much, we can rent other space. However, if they have a monopoly in an area, that could present a real problem.

What we do need to worry about, and do something about, is when they gain control of more and more of our key industries.

Their moves into biotechnology, the aircraft industry (they will produce some 20% of the new Boeing 777), and the auto industry which is also a key part of our defense industry. The whole high tech computer industry with all its ramifications in the military and other strategic areas as well as the infiltration of our education system would be most dangerous to our country.

In conclusion we have seen the great strengths of Japan. The great threat to America of their long range plan of world economic domination. How gullible we have been in being brainwashed as to their true motives. Their plan is set and in action. It's up to us to stop it before it's too late. Hopefully, we still have some time.

In the following chapters I will make some suggestions on how we can hopefully regain control of our future. ▫

Section III:

How We Can Still Win The War After Losing So Many Battles

WE NEED TO *have our government show leadership in the commercial and trade area and move quickly and aggressively as President Bush has done in a political and military way in the Gulf and Panama. We must abandon the weak kneed approach of the past that let the Tojos, Hitlers, Stalins, and others cause havoc in the world.*

In commerce we must fight the approach of the old Colonial empires which Japan is reincarnating in a new modern way.

We saw in Section II how Japan is causing havoc in an economic way. But we have let them. It's our fault as much as theirs for not waking up to what is happening.

In Section III, I will discuss some actions that we can take to prepare the way for the solutions in Section IV.

This will require controlling the Japanese lobbyists (Chapter 10), learning from Japanese mistakes (Chapter 11), and learning how to deal effectively with Japan as an equal not on a bended knee (Chapter 12). Then, equally, if not more importantly, we must develop our own efficient manufacturing industries, just like we have developed the world's most advanced military industries (Chapter 13). Then we can re-enter the world markets competitively and serve our own domestic markets with quality goods. □

Chapter 10:

TOUGHENING GOVERNMENT OFFICIALS AND COUNTERING THE POWERFUL JAPANESE LOBBY

FOR YEARS OUR government officials have been unable to look out for our best interests because:

1) They were told to be nice to Japan because it was a developing nation, and from a military security standpoint, we didn't want to upset them because of their proximity to the U.S.S.R. **The geo-politicians have dominated our policy, not business people or economists.**

2) Our trade negotiators were changing assignments every couple of years while the Japanese had the same people at the negotiating table for decades. Our people were simply outgunned by highly competent Japanese negotiators.

Some of our negotiators have also had other strikes against them:

1) Too many negotiators with legal backgrounds instead of business. They may be famous lawyers, well known politicians, or former government officials but inexperienced in the real long range trade area compared to the Japanese. The legal approach is not big in Japan. Always remember we probably have more lawyers south of 14th Street in New York than there are in all Japan.

2) Too little knowledge of the areas being negotiated.

3) Concern that a strong position will hurt their chances to become a Japanese lobbyist.

4) Concern that a tough position will cause the Japanese to retaliate.

5) Lack of experience and understanding in working with

the Japanese or even in international business.

6) No guts or courage. They don't believe "you need to rock the boat" to get results.

In 1982, I warned Douglas Newkirk, a newly minted assistant trade representative, about how he would have to negotiate with the Japanese, "Don't be confused by all the bowing, the courtesies, the geisha parties. Forget that. Stick to your negotiating. You are holding all the cards. (But) unless someone hits them over the head, your negotiations are going to be worthless."

You need to embarrass the Japanese publicly to get any favorable action. There are many examples of this noted through this book. We now know all of our trade negotiations have had very little useful effect. In fact, our trade deficit with Japan increased many fold as the years went by.

The Japanese negotiators don't have these weaknesses!! This is why they win and we lose!! And our trade deficit increased from $21 billion in 1981 to over $50 billion in 1989.

We see the big headlines in May 1991 that our trade deficit is at an 8 year low. Our top government officials take credit for this good news. But if you look at the figures you see that our trade deficit with Japan increased from **$3.57** billion in March 1990 to **$3.58** billion in March 1991. And our trade deficit with Japan increased from $3.16 billion in February 1991 to $3.58 billion in March 1991. Not much progress when you also add in the increased imports from satellite Japanese plants in other Southeast Asian countries which don't show up in these figures.

It was this obvious lack of support from our trade officials that caused me to turn down the opportunity, in 1984, to head up the U.S. Commerce Department operation at the American Embassy in Tokyo.

Herb Cochran, the U.S. Commercial Attache in Tokyo, who had been so helpful in working with us to overcome some of the barriers to our trade with Japan, urged me to consider the position when I retired from AMF that year.

Also, Clyde Prestowitz, apparently at the recommendation of Cochran, asked me to consider the position. These two men have been our most able and outspoken advocates of correcting our trade relations with Japan. Prestowitz, a former trade negotiator, has had the courage to speak out to such a degree that the Japanese call him one of the "Gang of Four." The Japanese must be very upset that such an able government official couldn't be made a Japanese lobbyist.

Even with the support of such fine able people, I didn't consider the position because, even with a staff of 37 people in Tokyo, we would get frustrated with no real support from Washington.

You can see a parallel to this problem when you look at the Vietnam War that was run by politicians in Washington instead of the military as in the Gulf War where we let the military run the war. Until the war was stopped! And the mess ensued.

I am confident if able people, like Prestowitz and Cochran, could have called some of the shots on Japanese trade negotiation instead of faceless people in Washington you would see totally different results today.

It is always interesting to note the flurry of favorable pronouncements from the Japanese just before a major international meeting. We see this two or three times a year and we see it again in June 1991. Just before the meeting in London of the Group of Seven, Prime Minister Kaifu or some Japanese official announces they will **probably** open up **bidding** on Japanese construction projects to American companies. (That doesn't mean you can get a contract—only bid.)

They then announce they **may** lift the ban on rice imports. The Japanese just want all the American officials to know how nice the Japanese are when they meet in London. Of course, part of this movement by the Japanese in this case is a reaction to the heat they have been getting from us on construction and rice. But don't expect much to happen after the G-7 meeting unless we stay tough. In the past, we haven't and business went on as usual.

When we look at the earlier agreement with the Japanese on construction and on integrated circuits (semi-conductors) we note that very few results were achieved, as was pointed out by U.S. Trade Representative Yeutter. We also find that there were many other hidden barriers beyond the agreements.

Even when we hear very strong talk from our government such as in 1982, that the Reagan Administration was planning a major trade offensive against Japan, it soon evaporated in thin air. They even talked of reciprocity. Some powerful influence must have shot that down in flames as our trade deficit increased another $30 billion/year in the next few years. It must have been a very weak offensive.

The best possible course to toughen government officials is to first try and get each administration to put people with the proper experience and knowledge in these trade positions and keep them there for many years with bi-partisan support. Our old "on the job training" approach is not working.

Secondly, we have to put some restrictions on the future employment of former government officials. None of this little "slap on the wrist" one year delay in becoming a lobbyist.

For example:
- Ban all government officials (elected or appointed) from working for a foreign power or foreign company for 10 years after government service. If, as some potential lobbyists claim, that would be unfair as they wouldn't have very many other job opportunities, the situation only points out how much control Japan has over us.
- Tighten foreign agent registration to include all PR firms and law firms who have clients that engage the firms to lobby on their behalf. The firms should be treated the same as individual foreign agents.

- Hire Pat Choate to update his lobbyist and foreign agent list each year and publish it in the Congressional Record and in major newspapers so the American people know which people are not working for the interests of America but for some foreign power or entity.
- Follow an old traditional diplomatic procedure. Japan will be permitted to have exactly the same number of agents and lobbyists in America as we have in Japan.

Above all we must have some courage and common sense so that we don't believe the propaganda of the Japanese hirelings that horrible things will happen if we irritate the Japanese. And if there is a short term cost to countering the Japanese economic invasion, we must be willing to pay it to avoid long term ecomonic domination.

You always have to remember if a trade war develops with Japan **they will lose $50 billion a year in favorable trade balance.** Sure, we will be hurt in some areas where we export to them but they still lose $50 billion and the **Japanese are too smart** to let that happen in spite of veiled threats.

We would of course have some real problems. We might have to go back to work and manufacture cars, trucks and all kinds of things and take the workers out of Burger King, McDonald's, the brokerage houses, etc. and put them in some real **manufacturing** work, at **better** wages.

This may sound too tough for some people but you may recall some people were considered naive or even "bashers" when they cautioned us about Hitler or Saddam Hussein but were later proven quite correct. □

Chapter 11:

THE JAPANESE ARE NOT PERFECT: LET'S LEARN FROM THEIR MISTAKES

THE JAPANESE AND their hirelings have done an excellent job of brainwashing many Americans people into thinking they are perfect. They don't make mistakes. They don't make imperfect products.

But those of us who have worked closely with Japan are aware of quite a different story.

For years when I worked in Asia, the message was that the Japanese cars were good for 3 years but get rid of them then before big problems developed.

Later we saw that when Honda started exporting cars to America, they had great problems as they rusted away.

Even as late as 1990, I kept hearing reports that in the Northern states, where we use a lot of salt on the roads in the winter, the Subarus were referred to as "rust buckets."

Then in 1990, when the Lexus LS-400 came on the market with great fanfare, (an excellent copy of the BMW 750) but at half the price, it was recalled with three significant defects. The most dangerous was that the cruise control could malfunction and it would stay in cruise after you attempted to turn it off.

We saw in the J.D. Power 1990 New Car Initial Quality Survey Buick was rated #5 after some fine Japanese and German cars but with Buick rated better than Hondas, Nissan, Acura and Mazda.

We see the Suzuki Samurai named as a most dangerous car because it rolls over so easily.

We see the courts awarding damages to people hurt or killed in apparently defective Japanese cars. But it all seems very quiet compared to the publicity when it's a problem with an American car.

In other areas, we hear of the serious problems with the Japanese manufactured L-tryptophan, a dietary supplement, that apparently is the cause of a rare and potentially fatal blood disorder.

So, while the Japanese make many excellent products, they are not as infallible as we are often led to believe.

But we can learn from these Japanese mistakes. I often call it the Japanese secret!

The Japanese secret is that when they make mistakes, and they do make many, they **quickly work to solve the problem,** instead of passing the blame on to others.

In America, we have started to put great emphasis on quality which is very good. But unfortunately we think of quality as just making good products. The Japanese know that is important but even more important is **service,** or as the Japanese call it **after service.** This is where many American companies fall down. And it's just not the big manufacturers. It's just as often the small manufacturers or retailers who fail in this area.

Even a mediocre product can do well in the market place if the **after service** is good. We saw that with our competitors in Japan who had a product that was quite inferior to our product as well as the product of our other American competitor. America should learn the importance of **after service.**

We saw the importance of this in the introduction of one of our electrical mechanical machines in over 60 countries around the world. We guaranteed service in most countries of the world in 24 hours (in some in 48 hours due to distance) or their annual minimum rent would be reduced. Many people thought we were being unrealistic to make such a guarantee but it wasn't a great burden due to some advance planning. Every customer was required to send their technicians to one of our schools for a three week course prior to installing the equipment. We had schools in the U.S.A., Germany, UK, Japan, Hong Kong, Australia and Sweden and taught in at least eight languages.

Every customer also had to purchase a spare parts kit. This service and training (organized by Art Smith, our Director of Service) was undoubtedly our most powerful sales tool as we gained 60-70% and even 100% of the business in many countries most years. Salesmen are great, but quality and after service is even greater. The Japanese know this very well.

The Japanese have a much bigger problem than improving quality which they have solved quite well. I call this their "one track railroad mentality." They become so sure that some business, some idea or some venture is so good that they speed down that "one track railroad" right over the cliff. We saw that in 1970 and you still see some repeats today.

When we were building bowling centers in Japan in 1970, we saw serious overbuilding taking place. At that time, we had about 15 million active bowlers and they had about 25 hours of TV bowling shows a week. At that time, there were about 70,000 bowling lanes in Japan. About one half as many as the United States, but they had only about one half as many people.

We became very concerned when they kept adding more at a fast rate. So we stopped all sales on credit except for the three or four giant 'Zaibatsu' trading Companies. We felt this was the strongest message that we could send by insisting they could only buy for cash.

But that didn't stop them. The sales increased until in the next three years we doubled the number of lanes in Japan. We sold about another half a billion dollars of equipment for cash. The Japanese were in such a rush to get equipment that in the fall of 1972 they pressured us to airlift the equipment to Japan. I arranged to charter 32 Stretch DC-8 aircraft from Flying Tigers and Japan Airlines to fly to Japan lumber, machines and equipment. The demand was so great that for us to ship 20,000 machines to Japan that year we ran all U.S. plants 24 hours a day seven days a week.

We even had our UK plant working at full capacity to help out. That year we got the "Queen's Award for Industry" as a top exporter from the UK to Japan. The demand for American maple lumber was so great the U.S. Commerce Department would call me up once a week to try and find out what we were paying for maple. It seems this was causing problems to the furniture industry as all of the top quality maple was going to Japan.

But finally there were just not enough bowlers to go around. (The market reached a top of about 25 million bowlers). Then came the crash as the business started to collapse and many Japanese companies went down that "one track railroad" right over the cliff.

That year (1972) the total capital investment in bowling in Japan (including the land, buildings and equipment) exceeded the total investment in the **Japanese Automobile Industry** according to a business report.

The crash was so swift and deep that we started buying back the used equipment (and some was brand new—the center never opened) for $200 a lane and machine. This was the equipment that we had sold a year or two earlier for $20,000 cash per lane and machine. We exported this used equipment all over the world.

The two Japanese manufacturers who had 30% of the market at the end effectively went out of business. They had made a classic error, **failing to develop world markets.** Many American companies make this same mistake of developing only their domestic market and not the world markets.

When the Japanese failed to heed our warnings that the market was reaching a saturated level, they illustrated another shortcoming. As I see it, their arrogance makes them "too smart to listen" to US "gaijin's" (that's us). That failure is another of their true Achilles heels.

As we now observe their excesses in real estate and in their stock market (which is already down some 30%) from early 1990 we may see further crashes in other areas. If the American people respond to some of the suggestions in the last chapter, it will probably cause some other crashes due to Japanese excesses.

We also see other mistakes by the Japanese in their drive for world domination.

But probably the biggest mistake the Japanese are making is their pushy, arrogant attack on the world markets with little or no respect for other people in the world. I am afraid the Japanese are blinded by their success. They have not realized that you can push people only so far before they react. We only have to look at recent history in Eastern Europe, USSR, China and other areas of the world.

This point was well noted by the new lady Prime Minister of France, Edith Cresson in 1991. She has been quoted as saying, "Japan is an adversary that doesn't play by the rules and has an absolute desire to conquer the world. You have to be naive or blind not to recognize that."

It's good to know that there are people in high places in the world who are very aware of what is happening in international trade.

Let's all learn from Japan's mistakes. □

Chapter 12:
DEALING WITH— AND MAKING DEALS WITH THE JAPANESE

THIS MAY SOUND like a very bold title for a chapter after you recall the hundreds of articles in the media about how difficult it is to do business in Japan.

I do not pretend to have any magic formula or unique insight into dealing with the Japanese. **All I know is what the Japanese taught me.** Much of this is a review of my own experiences of what worked and what didn't. I also had an excellent opportunity over 40+ years to study how they treat each other, both companies and individuals.

I will try to explain the elements in Japan that are quite different from what I encountered elsewhere in the world.

Then I will note the techniques that we used to try and put us on a more even footing in our dealings so as not to be the underdog, which is so common.

This will be followed by an examination of a number of experiences that we had that illustrate the Japanese approach to a particular problem and how it was resolved on a fair basis. Not how our government trade negotiations have been going on for years—A few small gains and many large losses so that our trade deficit kept growing.

UNDERSTANDING THE JAPANESE
1) Logic—
You soon realize that the Japanese analysis of a situation may follow a completely different logic than you would expect. An example: Mr. Morita commented in a speech he made some time ago that we Americans often act out of emotionalism. This

is alluded to in the Japanese version of the *Japan That Can Say No* where he complained that the U.S. Government acted improperly in banning the sale of some Toshiba products in America after Toshiba was cited for selling machines with secret technology to Russia in violation of the COCOM agreement.

He is reported to have said that this action by the U.S. Government was a violation of the U.S. Constitution since it was a law that we passed retroactively to the crime. It also violated our constitution in that it didn't give Toshiba an opportunity to defend itself.

I guess if I were to follow the same logic as Mr. Morita it was **unconstitutional for America to declare war on Japan** after they attacked Pearl Harbor. That was clearly an action we took retroactively after that crime. But we did give them the opportunity to defend themselves retroactively.

So when you see this unusual logic in Japan don't be surprised —it is only a rationalization to prove they are right and you are wrong.

2) Small Profit Margins—

This comes as a shock to many western business people. We encountered this in our own joint venture operations when the Japanese said the J.V. was making too much profit. This was pointed out to us very clearly. One year when their 50% of the profit from our joint venture was paid to the Japanese parent, it represented a very significant share of their profit. And their Japanese parent company had sales of almost 200 times the sale of our J.V.!!

Of course, there are also other reasons why the Japanese often work on such small profit margins. They have many people down the line of a complex distribution chain, all of whom have to make a profit. Some of these people may have some connections in one way or another with the basic manufacturing company, which gives them some leverage.

Also working on much smaller margins than we would ever consider makes them very competitive in the world markets.

3) Long term planning and thinking—

This point has been made so many times I am almost tired of hearing it. But it is very real, and very important to anyone's success. And we haven't learned it yet.

4) Land Costs—

The Japanese approach to and treatment of land costs in their financial analysis of a project is most unusual. I am not sure I ever successfully explained this to our New York headquarters. When I first started working in Japan, I attempted to do our normal profit and loss and cash flow analysis on each proposed project. I encountered a major problem—the land cost. We were all aware of the high cost of land in Japan. Yet, when I looked out the window of the New Japan Hotel in the Akasaka section of Tokyo, I could see this small auto body repair shop across the street on this large piece of very valuable land. When I discussed this situation with potential Japanese customers they quickly pointed out that I didn't understand Japan. They told me you never put the cost of land in your financial analysis as they treat that separately. As you know, the value of land always goes up. In other words, the land was not thought of as part of the project—it was a separate project.

Once we understood this unusual approach, good things started to happen. After all, who were we to change Japanese thinking?

When you see relatively new buildings torn down to make way for other uses of the land, you soon realize that the land is important, but what you put on it is not important and it is quite separate.

However, when I tried to convince our management to let our J.V. buy five acres of land in Totsuka with an old building and a pond from Johnson and Johnson for a quarter of a million dollars an acre in 1969 they thought it was outrageous. When they heard that during the fall typhoon season it was often under two or three feet of water they expressed even greater concern. But we did buy it and put up a $1 million warehouse/office. A few years later we sold off this $2.5 investment for about $12 million, and the building was not considered of any great value.

5) Quality and after service—

These are relative new terms to the Japanese. In my earlier years in Japan, I saw very little of either. But when they realized the importance of these two points, they adopted them with a vengeance. This point illustrates how quickly quality and service can be improved. We can do it also once our management and labor understand. Fortunately, we have many companies who have always understood their importance. And more are learning quickly. But we have to remember that quality alone will not solve the problem. You must have excellent and rapid service (or afterservice as it is known in Japan).

TECHNIQUES

Again, I must thank the Japanese for teaching me what techniques to use in dealing with them successfully.

1) Be accurate, firm and have notes to back up the past.

I know this sounds very simplistic. If I hadn't seen so many negotiations fail because people didn't follow these simple rules, I would never mention them. Several things usually happen sooner or later.

First, you can be sure that after each day's discussions one or more of the Japanese side will work late into the night preparing a summary of the day's discussions. This summary will be presented at the start of the next day's discussions and both sides are expected to agree to the summary and sign it. Many times it is a reasonably accurate document, but, as often as not, it has a slant on it favoring the Japanese side. Whether this is intentional or just a language problem I am not sure. But study it carefully before you agree.

2) Have proper people at meetings.

You have heard businessmen complain for years that when they meet there are 10 Japanese and two Westerners. In fact, that is true through most of Asia. We often complain that we are outnumbered and negotiations take so long. But what many people don't understand is that the time for negotiations is long but the time to put the total project into operation is short.

All those Japanese at the meeting represented every function that would eventually be necessary to make the project work. During the negotiations they understood why each point was agreed upon. And they were a party to the agreement.

The foreigners, however, usually only have two or three people at the meetings. Then, when the final agreement is reached, they have to go home and sell the idea to all the people who must make it work. Some of the people will never understand why some point was agreed. This may result in less than enthusiastic support.

On the other hand, all the Japanese on the project are already committed and they move very quickly with no more internal discussion or dissent. This is a technique we could well afford to learn on any proposed project.

3) Put on the defense—solicit apologies—embarrass publicly.

These techniques are quite different than I have found in other countries. They are also much more innocent and kinder than they sound.

When I would arrive late at our Totsuka office/warehouse in the morning from Tokyo, I would stop and speak to our President, Mr. Watanabe. I would innocently say I was sorry to be late for the meeting but the traffic on the SHUTO expressway was terrible. As an American we would probably respond that's a terrible road, I don't know when our dumb government is going to fix it. But not the Japanese. They feel **personally** responsible and embarrassed if something is wrong in Japan.

The next morning I innocently said I missed seeing Mount Fuji in the morning. It's all blocked out with smog. Years ago, when I would drive to Haneda each morning it was such a beautiful sight to see snowcapped Mount Fuji. Again, there was great personal concern that Japan had let the smog get so bad that we could no longer see this beautiful mountain except on rare days. In America we would just blame someone else for the bad situation. We would feel no reason to apologize.

I soon found that having the Japanese apologize for something each morning was a good way to start the day. I didn't plan it that way, they just taught me.

Over the years if you have had personal experiences or you follow the stories on Japan in the media, you soon realize that about the only time they give in to any serious complaint is after they have been **embarrassed publicly.**

I personally saw that in the baseball bat issue, in the Hatteras Yacht situation I mentioned in Chapter 4, and here in 1991 when they were embarrassed publicly by our government, particularly Congress, for not paying up on the Gulf War situation. Then in June 1991, there was a world outcry about the rare Hawkbill turtles that were being cut up for jewelry. Only after President Bush and some wildlife groups put the pressure on them publicly did they agree to stop the industry. They never give an inch unless you force them.

4) **Keep your eyes open to see when they are about ready to make a big mistake and go over the cliff. (The one track mind syndrome).**

I have mentioned earlier in Chapter 11 that in spite of our warnings, they kept buying so much bowling equipment that the industry became so saturated it collapsed.

We have quietly observed them doing the same in their stock market. Many of us noted a year ago when the Nikkei Average was over 35,000 and P/E Ratios were up in the 60's and 70's that they were about to go over the cliff.

As of June 1991, I understand the Japanese stock market will have to go up by about 60% to reach old highs.

Just be careful and don't get caught up in their euphoria. It's costly. So the technique is **beware.**

These are just a few of the techniques we have learned in dealing successfully with Japanese.

ILLUSTRATIVE CASE STUDIES AND TECHNIQUES IN ACTION

Our 50-50 Joint Venture

In 1960, working very closely with some of the staff (Clyde Wakatake, Ken Watanabe and Suzy Kitagawa) of our 100% owned AMF Japan, we pressed on to sell bowling in Japan. We were able to sell three projects to Korakuen Stadium, Funabashi Center and Kanebo Silk. We arranged for these to be imported by Mitsubishi as our agent. The equipment was to be sold directly to the customers and the machinery to be the property of AMF Japan and leased. At that time, we would only lease the machinery.

After reviewing this potential new market with Frank White, the President of AMF's International Operations, and his new assistant, Merlin Nelson, we decided that we probably needed a partner in Japan to really develop the market. We also knew that we could only have a maximum of 50% of the new venture as the Japanese had tightened up the laws on foreign companies since we had formed our 100% owned company in Japan some years earlier.

When Merlin and I went to Japan in early 1961, he suggested some key points that should be pursued from the contract point of view, which was his expertise.

I suggested a number of points that should be pursued from the product and operations point of view which was my area of experience.

I felt Merlin completely shocked the Japanese when we approached the potential Japanese partners. First, he explained to each of these potential partners that we were going to approach four companies—Mitsubishi, Sumitumo, Marubeni, and C. Itoh. This openness startled the Japanese.

We carried out detailed discussions for about three weeks to try and determine whom we felt was the most capable partner and equally who would actively support this Joint Venture. We did not want to have them just add another name to their list of foreign partners.

Then Merlin quietly advised each potential partner that since we were bringing much more to the Venture than they were, we would require, in addition to the 50-50 split of the profits, a management fee of three percent of the gross revenues.

This seemed very insignificant. At the time I was preparing various five year projections of the operations, none of which indicated revenues of over $10 to $15 million per year. No one ever dreamed that later our revenues would reach $258 million per year and this management fee would be nearly $8 million per year.

Later, we used this same principle in other Joint Ventures where we did not have majority control.

Another key point in the agreement was that the Joint Venture would purchase products from our company at the same distributor prices that we sold to our other subsidiaries or distributors. That was a price list that we had developed to keep the import authorities in many countries satisfied that our intercompany pricing was at arms length. Also it complied with the guidelines set by the Internal Revenue Service on intercompany pricing. No one could have imagined the favorable impact this had on our U.S., U.K., and Swedish manufacturing plants in the years to come. (The only reason we had to export to Japan from U.K. and Sweden was that our U.S. plants couldn't meet the demand.)

Another key point in the JV was that we would sell directly to the end user and not go through any distribution network.

What kept the Joint Venture successful in addition to the rapid growth of business, was that the people from AMF and C. Itoh who negotiated the agreement actively worked with the JV regardless of their other advancements in their companies for the 15 years of the JV. You can't keep changing the people responsible for a Joint Venture if you want it to succeed.

While we were working on the Joint Venture discussions, we had a request from our customer, Mr. Tanabe of Korakuen Stadium. Since his new building for the 60 lane center was not complete, he wanted to open a smaller center in an existing building. We already had the equipment in Japan that we had asked Mitsubishi to import for us.

The plan was to convert the Korakuen Skating Rink into an eight lane center so they could open the first automated center in Japan. We were pleased with the idea as we had made it a policy to be first in every country around the world.

There was a problem however. Some of the people at Korakuen wanted us to put this modern equipment in this old building with few modifications to the building.

Realizing this I made up a list of **15** conditions outlining what they had to do to the building before we could agree to their request.

Nelson and I got on the subway and went to Korakuen to discuss the plan. It was important that we arrived by subway as all Japanese thought all Americans were rich and rode around in chauffeur driven cars.

We explained that they had to completely re-do the building to include air conditioning, acoustical ceilings, carpeted floors, a new entrance and lobby, etc. If they did all that work to our satisfaction, we would install the equipment and later remove it and put it in the new building when it was ready. Needless to say we met considerable resistance. But our position was clear; we had to introduce this new sport to Japan on a first class basis or we wouldn't do it. This was probably one of Japan's first lessons in **quality.** It also had a great impact for years to come as every new center had to be as good or better than the first. We always felt that the standards we set that Saturday morning in Tokyo had a great influence in causing some 25 million people to take up the sport in the next few years.

Korakuen went on to buy millions of dollars of equipment from us. Mr. Tanabe always remembered our early meetings and our insistence on quality and a good image, as he reminded me at my retirement party some 25 years later.

- *Clear Understanding—*

One of the most important elements in dealing with the Japanese is to be sure that you thoroughly understand each others positions. This is difficult in any venture but it is compounded in Japan by their language and culture.

Ray Jessup who was our senior man in the Joint Venture (Executive VP of the Joint Venture) did an excellent job of ensuring that this principle was carried out. Jessup organized board meetings each month. These were really operation meetings where a broad range of subjects were openly discussed. They were always well attended by all of the local directors as well as AMF directors from the U.S.A. and C. Itoh directors, from Mr. Eikichi Itoh, the Chairman of C. Itoh, to other C. Itoh senior managing directors who were also directors of the JV.

To ensure that all of our discussions were well documented and understood, Jessup tape recorded the entire meeting. Since there were conversations in both English and Japanese, the tape gave him the ability to get it all translated and reduced to a detailed report. I must point out this was an interesting, valuable document. **Not the typical canned Board of Director Minutes.**

This also let any director who could not attend have an excellent report on the company.

This action, plus Jessup's routine of keeping us informed of any possible problem, permitted us to arrange a meeting with Mr. Itoh or other key Itoh person to solve a problem quickly. These board meeting reports proved most valuable to us when the market was booming just before the crash.

We had insisted that all sales could be made only on a cash basis due to our concern about overbuilding in the industry. Itoh agreed. We also insisted that sizable down payments be made at the time of accepting an order. We were concerned that, if a crash came, we might get many cancellations and we would be hit with cancellation costs for all the equipment in the pipeline. This was all carefully documented at a board meeting, since I had insisted I could not place more orders on the manufacturing plants, if the Joint Venture would not be responsible for cancellation costs if they occurred.

As expected, cancellations did occur. We then learned that the C. Itoh staff at the JV had returned the down payments to many customers without our knowledge. The JV had to cancel many orders for products and were hit with large cancellation costs. But armed with the board minutes, where all the above points were noted as well as the statements by the C. Itoh people's demanding that I place more orders on the plants and rush the equipment to keep the customers satisfied, we had a **basis for discussion.**

The C. Itoh side finally agreed that we had warned them of this potential problem and paid us a few million dollars in cancellation costs.

You always have to be very exact, correct and detailed in dealing with the Japanese.

■ *Getting the Attention of the Japanese—*

When the boom ended, we had several customers who had purchased equipment on long terms who still had a balance due. Fortunately, on most of these projects, we not only had the equipment as security, but also had secondary security. These secondary securities ranged from a cruise ship, to mansions (apartment houses), to land. A few customers, however, had very little or no secondary security and the old equipment had virtually no value.

Even though the Japanese are probably the most honorable people I have known in paying their debts, we still had some problems.

We sent Po Mar, from our business development department in our New York office to Japan to take up the position of Vice President to help collect these debts. He set up a very excellent program that was most effective.

As I mentioned earlier in the book, to get action from the Japanese you must first **get their attention.** You can say something to have them apologize. You can embarrass them publicly, and so forth.

In this case the decision was made to go to court and sue the customers for non-payment. It was pointed out to me that the Japanese courts would probably never make a decision on our lawsuits.

If the court were to make a decision, it would have to say one party is wrong and one is right. That is rarely done in the Japanese culture.

So much to the frustration of many of us initially, until we understood the procedure, very little happened. At each hearing, the Judge would ask the parties if they had settled their dispute. The parties would say they hadn't. The Judge would then suggest that the parties go and have some more discussions to resolve the matter and come back in three months to report to the Judge.

Eventually, we would resolve the matter and so advise the Judge. But the plan was most effective as we did get the **attention** of the debtor and we did **embarrass** them enough to solve the problem.

In previous chapters I have given other examples of how you embarrass the Japanese publicly: the Hatteras Yachts (Chapter 11) and Nakasone's Market Access Proamples of how you embarrass the Japanese publicly: the Hatters Yachts (Chapter 11) and Nakasone's Market Access Promotion Committee (Chapter 11), and the baseball bat issue.

In each of these cases, the Japanese acted positively after the public embarrassment.

If you recall their beliefs (as discussed in Chapter 2) about being the superior race, you can understand why they find it most difficult to handle criticism.

- *Buying back the Joint Venture—*

By the time we considered buying back our partner's 50% of the Joint Venture, we had 30 years of experience of dealing with the Japanese. We had enjoyed wonderful success in Japan and had worked with some of the most able people of any country in the world. Our relationships were very good and very solid.

The U.S. news magazines would approach me when I arrived in Tokyo, asking what the problem was that caused us to end our Joint Venture with C. Itoh. They would ask the same questions of Frank Chillrud, our Corporate Treasurer in New York.

The reporters worked very hard trying to develop a negative story.

On one occasion when I was in Tokyo and a reporter kept pressing me for a negative story, I told him there was no problem. Our Joint Venture had enjoyed a most successful 15 years and its mission was accomplished. When he kept on pressing me for a negative story on the ending of the Joint Venture, I suggested that if he didn't believe me, why didn't he join Mr. Itoh and me for lunch. Then he could see first hand that we had no problems and we were very good friends.

I guess it was too much for him to have to confront the truth and he wouldn't join us for lunch. This publication then went on to publish a story that I recall **questioned** why we ended the Joint Venture.

During the discussions to terminate the Joint Venture, a number of interesting things developed that illustrated some key points in dealing with the Japanese.

Why the Japanese Government Works So Closely With Business.

When we had decided that the Joint Venture was no longer needed, I was authorized to go to Japan and start discussions with our partners. It was the desire of our management to sell our 50%, even though I thought we should buy our partner's 50%. It had been pointed out to me that since we had written down and disposed of the JV surplus inventory and since we had set up extensive reserves to cover the costs of winding down the JV plus some old bad debt reserves, we had a large tax loss for the year.

Our financial people explained to me that would be very valuable to C. Itoh if they purchased our 50% of the JV.

So off I went to Tokyo to sell the JV. During the first morning's discussions, I outlined our position and pointed out the value of the JV and the extra value of the tax loss to Itoh.

Then to my surprise, Mr. Yamasaki, a Senior Managing Director of C. Itoh, turned to me and said to the effect, yes, we understand the value of the tax loss but we would never use it. It would not be fair to our government to claim a tax loss after all the great success we have enjoyed in this venture over the last 15 years.

I called our management in New York to explain this startling position of our partners. I'm sure our New York tax experts thought I had misunderstood our partners. No one had ever heard of a company freely giving up a very proper tax loss which would lower their taxes due their government.

Finally, I was given permission to negotiate the purchase of the JV since Itoh didn't feel it was nearly as valuable as I had suggested. A very interesting switch to be sure. One day you are selling and the next day buying.

Other Negotiating Tactics.

During the ensuing negotiations, a few more interesting insights on dealing with the Japanese developed.

The first was noted as we tried to value the assets. These were mainly land, buildings and receivables. We first worked on the land and buildings. Over the several months of our discussions, we resolved them all except the value of the warehouse/office building at Totsuka. This was a fine building with piling 100 feet deep to support it's three stories. It was a fine building except for the ground floor in the warehouse. The sections of floor were not tied into the structure but were floated on the ground between the girders. Since this was very marshy land, they kept sinking. Twice we had filled in the sinking floor with six to 10 inches of asphalt. But it kept sinking.

The negotiations finally got down to the point that all was settled except "the sinking floor at Totsuka." We had pointed out that the other new buildings that we had been responsible for at the Chiba site some 60 miles from Totsuka were fine. It was only the building that Itoh's contractors had built at Totsuka that had a problem.

To finally settle the problem, it was agreed that all the directors and key people from Itoh would personally inspect the Totsuka building.

Our American staff at the JV organized the tour. All people were met in the lobby and issued hard hats to proceed through this dangerous ground floor. There were special cat walks between the girders with warning signs to guide you over the sunken floor sections. It was a very dramatic event.

I can only guess that they were apparently embarrassed as we quickly settled the value of the building.

A Small Lesson in Labor Relations.

We had already resolved the personnel termination situation. While doing that, we once again exploded the myth of life time employment in Japan.

At the peak of our operations, it was estimated we had about 10,000 people working for us. But in good Japanese fashion about 9,700 of these were contract personnel. Only about 300 were on our payroll and directly employed by us. For a $258 million business that is a very interesting figure. Sales of about $800,000 per employee.

The contract personnel were not only the construction workers, which is common in many countries, but they also were most of the workers in our warehouses and factories. The majority of all the workers on the payroll were sales and administrative people. So it's very easy in Japan to keep most of your workers on your payroll during a drop in your business. You just let the contract people go. I have never figured out what happens to all of the poor contract workers in Japan.

The employees on our **payroll** that had to be terminated were paid three times the amount required by the government in appreciation of the great work they had performed over the years.

THE J-Vs-J AFFAIR—

This affair offered a most interesting insight into Japanese thinking as it was a battle between two Japanese companies. We were on the sidelines, but as a very interested party.

It all started when this very strong minded owner of a number of retail stores invested in a new business—too late. His last center opened just after the crash in the bowling market. Since the Joint Venture was not extending credit, the JV had sold the equipment to a large trading company who sold it to this customer.

To try and get out of a bad investment, he then filed court actions, both civil and criminal, against the trading company with all kinds of groundless claims. (I say groundless because in personal discussions with the gentleman, it became clear that his only real request regarding the equipment was to remove a new modification to the equipment so it would be like his older equipment. This we agreed to do). His real problem was that he had made a bad investment.

But in his apparent anger, he allegedly made all kinds of demands and threats, including bombing if the company didn't buy back not only the equipment but the land and building also.

We then saw how a major Japanese company was effectively brought to its knees by a small businessman. We were never able to confirm all the harassment and threats but we felt they were real when the JV was asked to help.

This small businessman then bought 8,000 shares of the trading company stock and asked that it be divided into single shares so he could have them register it in 8,000 individual names. (Later he bought 4,000 more shares). It was explained to me that such an action was severe criticism of a large trading company and that was bad for Japan.

As the annual meeting time got closer and the thought of 8,000 new stockholders being at the meeting was a great concern. The trading company at the time had only 15,000 stockholders before this request to add 8,000 more.

Later, there were stories in the Japanese newspapers regarding share splitting by gangsters. There was no indication it was related to this situation but it did add to the concern. The JV was then told that for moral and social reasons it had to help resolve this situation quickly even though it was only indirectly involved. The JV did assist in helping solve this problem so that the

8,000 shares were never registered in individual names and the trading company wasn't embarrassed.

It's too bad we never explained to T. Boone Pickens how you bring a major Japanese company to its knees. Although he was only working with a midsize company, they brought him to a situation where he sold out and left. The lesson is that they really play "hardball" with each other.

So if you have a real problem in dealing with Japan, just think about how they treat each other.

We have all heard a lot about the honorable mob or organized crime, the Yakuza, as they are known in Japan. I only mention them as they apparently have a reputation of disrupting stockholder meetings, or at least pose that threat. I'm sure that was in the minds of the trading company when the above problem developed. They are much more open than our mobs and even carry business cards. We have recently heard how they were involved with two of the largest investment houses in Japan (Nomura and Nikko). These investment houses reportedly admitted loaning some of the big crime bosses $100 million. They are famous for sending chills through most Japanese.

One time, when I was on a train from Hammamatsu to Tokyo, a large group of the Yakuza came into the same car where our Japanese company executive and I were sitting. They were all dressed in black suits, white shirts and black ties. My Japanese associate became very nervous and quickly left the car. I later found him in another car and he explained the Yakuza were apparently going to a funeral for a fallen comrade. He never explained his quick departure. But I could see the fear they put in him.

Other Japanese Tactics.

My last bit of advice in dealing with the Japanese is how you deal with the element of surprise. I had two very memorable experiences with this tactic of theirs.

When our Joint Venture had been working very successfully for many years, I had a real surprise. A gentleman from our partners company, whom I didn't know well, suddenly presented to me a document to completely revise the Joint Venture Agreement. I can only think that they must have felt Nelson out-negotiated them several years earlier and they were going to change everything in their favor with a new JV Agreement. I took a quick look at it and handed it back and said, "Sorry, the current agreement is fine and it has several years until termination."

I have often wondered who had given this person the O.K. to try such a tactic. How high up had it come from??

But the classic surprise came later. We had been negotiating **for about six months** to buy back the other 50% of the Joint Venture. It had been tough negotiating, but all was going well. Mr. Yamasaki, a Senior Managing Director of C. Itoh, who was their chief negotiator, was a great and pleasant person to work with. We were well advanced in the negotiations with only a few remaining points to be resolved when it struck.

That morning, after I arrived in Tokyo, we had an early meeting to review all the outstanding points in the pending agreement. But this time, in addition to Mr. Yamasaki and his normal staff in the room, there was a new person whom I had never seen before. He looked like the man in a picture I had seen—the Commander of Santo Tomas Prison Camp.

After about two hours of discussions, he started to talk very strongly. He said I was being very unfair in my dealings with Itoh. This went on for several minutes. Then he started to say your company is dealing in a very bad manner with C. Itoh. I also let this go on for awhile.

I then said it was all right to criticize me but to make those statements about our company is something I would not tolerate.

I turned to Mr. Yamasaki and said, "I'm very sorry that these negotiations have to end but we can't go on if this man represents your company's attitude. I have enjoyed working with you these last several months and I'm sorry it has to end this way."

I then stood up with my two associates, Po Mar and Bill Brennen and left the room.

We went back to the hotel and discussed the situation and went to lunch. As we came out of the restaurant after lunch, there was a large group of Japanese bowing very low, apologizing and suggesting we start negotiations again.

We never saw the person again and his subject was never mentioned.

So don't be surprised by surprise and have the courage to be firm. This was just one more last desperate attempt to get us to make some major last minute concessions. Again, I wonder who authorized such an action? Learn how to deal with surprises. ▫

Chapter 13:

PROTECTING AND DEVELOPING OUR MANUFACTURING INDUSTRIES

MOST IMPORTANTLY, DON'T do what so many of your fallen comrades did—Excuses —Excuses—Excuses. And maybe add in ignorance. Not only didn't they realize that:
1) They had to make a quality product,
2) They had to service the product,
3) They had to think long-term and improve the product or develop new products, and
4) They had to compete in the **Global** markets and not give them away to others (have you ever heard of a U.S. company of any size saying, I am not going to sell in New York or California?)

But they also had wonderful **Excuses** for not going **Global:**
1) "They speak a strange language,"
2) "They use funny money,"
3) "It's complicated,"
4) "It's easier to sell here at home,"
5) "The competition is too strong,"
6) "They have different electricity, or"
7) "It takes too long."

Then we have the **Real Reasons** why we are in trouble:
1) We are moving from a **manufacturing** to **service** economy (big trouble),
2) We only think short-term—must please Wall Street,
3) We are not well educated (keep thinking we can solve the problem by throwing money at it),
4) We don't save enough (big trouble),
5) Our bankers, etc., wasted our savings by bad loans to

countries and developers and got a big negative return (and we taxpayers have to bail them out) instead of sound loans to manufacturing,

6) We are **Fat** and **Happy**—our single biggest problem?

As a result of all this we let others take over the world and the U.S. markets and we are becoming experts in **Chapter 11** bankruptcy—a **service** industry.

We need to analyze the problem and put forth some sound proven solutions. As we read annual reports and news stories we note a few companies are doing this:

- Put experienced manufacturing, marketing and engineering people in charge of companies instead of some financial experts who know how to move money around but don't know how to make a quality product and sell it at a profit. Fortunately, we are seeing this happening in IBM, GM and GE, to mention a few, who realize the need for good technical and marketing people at the top.

Having been with a company that was taken over by financial experts and see it slip away, I know how serious the problem is. When I saw the "Bean Counters" run down my plan (Plan #50) to buy back surplus used machinery from Japanese customers at .01 on the $1.00 to increase our profits and market share and help protect our future, I realized the problem first hand. They said the plan didn't meet the criteria of their asset management plan.

Ten years later at my retirement party, a young accountant had done a study to show that by turning down "Plan #50" it had cost the company much of its very profitable rental income base, reducing its pre-tax profits by about $20 million a year, as well as reducing market share and potential profits associated with it. Now we realize why this company did not have the funds to develop new products and expand its market. It wasn't the **Japanese** who stopped us, it was Ourselves (and our "Bean Counters").

There are a number of things we can do to protect our industries at home, among them:

1) Western companies (not only U.S.) need to join together to combat Japan business/government cooperation in cutting edge technology. A few examples are IBM and Siemens in semiconductor chips, Phillips and Whirlpool in appliances, and RCA-Phillips-Thomson in high definition television.

2) Companies need to set up aggressive long-term exporting and overseas manufacturing efforts (fight the Japanese off shore). You can learn from IBM, Ford, Corning, GE, Boeing, Coca-Cola, PepsiCo, and others.

3) Modernize manufacturing, taking the short term hit for the long-term ability to survive. Capital availability is not the problem. The problem is short-sighted, domestic-market-oriented executives and greedy bankers. Intel is investing $1 billion in new plants to keep ahead.

4) Stop giving away technology. Biotechnology is in extreme danger of becoming a U.S. brainpower/Japan ownership joint venture. This is not good for the U.S. pharmaceutical, chemical or agricultural industries. The same goes for aircraft. Japan has been given 20% of the production of the New Boeing 777 Aircraft. With this goes the know-how to develop an industry.

5) Enforce patent laws (make the Japanese at least pay.) As I have mentioned in Chapter 7 it took Texas Instruments 21 years to get the Japanese to issue a patent (the basic Kilby Patent) which covered the basic technology for all integrated circuits. By then, the Japanese controlled the world markets using what might be called stolen technology. The Japanese apparently didn't feel it was stolen technology—they were just using it free until their government got around to issuing the patent.

6) Demand **total** reciprocity and be bold negotiators. U.S.

law firms can't use their name in Japan. We can't sell rice, etc. If that's their rule, copy them exactly in setting rules for Japanese imports and business practices in America.

7) Beat the Japanese into China and Eastern Europe. When we were setting up manufacturing ventures in China, they all had one goal, to combat Japan in the world markets. China loved it. There is a natural enmity between China and Japan and a natural affinity between China and United States.

In addition, China still has a visceral hatred for Japan and what the Japanese invasion did to the Chinese from 1937 to 1945. Although the Japanese have rewritten their history books to deny their actions, China still has good memories about how the U.S. helped them against Japan during that period. But they will forget it if we don't work with them.

8) The Western Europeans have enacted tough stances against the Japanese to try to keep Japan from getting the kind of a strangle hold they have on America. The new 1991 European agreement with Japan on cars limits imports to 1.2 million a year. The combination of imports and transports would be limited to about 16% of the market. This is a fraction of the Japanese share of the American car market. It sounds tough but that is what the Japanese do to so many European and American products in Japan. But the Japanese are clever, they don't generally put a quota on imports (except maybe rice). The Japanese depend on a whole maze of techniques from specifications, distributions, custom regulations, local trade associations, and so forth to achieve the same results.

9) Convince America, our people, and our buisnesses to make the correct moves, we must cut through the propa-

ganda of Japan's hirelings—that we are fed daily by some well meaning media—and get the facts correct. This propaganda has made many Americans feel inferior. They think our economy is a fraction the size of Japan. They think all our workers are inefficient compared to Japan. They think only Japan can make a good product. Recently, however, *The Economist*, possibly the best business magazine in the world, tried to correct some of this misinformation about America. Their article: **"Yes, you are a superpower,"** exploded many incorrect perceptions of Japan by Americans. They pointed out that in a recent poll in America 48% of our people thought Japan's economy is bigger than America's. In fact, it's **only half as big.**

Fact #2: It takes the average Japanese worker **one hour** to produce what an **American** can produce in **31 minutes.**

And what I feel is a key comment, "America's economy has weaknesses but it is a giant with a cold, not a pygmy with cancer."

Yes, we have many problems but we must stand up and fight.

10) Think long term not short term. I recall very vividly my first experiences when I went to Japan to sell our machinery in 1959. As a young man, I came home very excited about the possibilities only to have them dashed by our Chairman, Mr. Morehead Patterson.

He quickly pointed out to me that the Japanese worker was only paid $500 per year. At that rate of pay it was much cheaper for the Japanese to do the work by hand instead of renting one of our machines.

But fortunately, for me Mr. Patterson had a deep interest in all international markets and a great long term vision.

He gave me a fatherly tap on the shoulder and said, I don't see much short term hope for your work in Japan, but you may keep trying. Which I did.

Unfortunately, he passed away about a year later and never had a chance to see the results of his "OK, you can keep trying" as our sales of that equipment in Japan rose to a high of $258 million a year.

In the meantime, the wages in Japan continued to rise until they were approaching those in America.

The realization that most country's markets eventually develop like Japan, spurred us on to attack the potential markets in China, Southeast Asia and the rest of the world with great success.

It is always good news to see the reports that companies like Proctor and Gamble are buying Czechoslovakia's biggest soap company. It's also taking actions in Hungary and Poland to expand its distribution. The experience of many of us is that such overseas operations lead to a large expansion of exports from America to those countries and do not result in a loss of American exports. Proctor and Gamble is just one of the American companies taking actions in the world markets. This takes courage, foresight and staying power to be successful—but it pays.

What's important is that once American companies take that aggressive action to develop world markets, we are then free to import other products and not destroy our manufacturing base or our standard of living.

11) Another area in which all American companies must be most vigilant is when imported products are dumped on the American market.

We have here, in 1991, the alleged dumping of Japanese minivans in America. Fortunately, the American manufacturers of minivans protested to our government. Based on the evidence presented, our government has agreed to investigate these charges. Hopefully, we will not be faced with similar situations as in the past where the foreign lobbyists apparently exerted great pressure on the International Trade Commission, and it determined the foreign imports were not hurting American Industry. Only to learn a few months later, according to the Detroit News, a key member of that Commission took a high paying job with a Japanese auto maker.

The Japanese are very clever to avoid getting caught on dumping charges. One of their simplest techniques, that I have observed over the years, is to not sell the same product in America as they sell in Japan. I was always curious when we bought the **Nissan President** model in Japan at a very high price why it wasn't sold in America. This was also true with many other models. Then I came to realize that, in effect, with the high price in Japan on one model they could use those profits to subsidize another model (only sold in America) so it could be exported to America at a very low price. This makes it most difficult to prove dumping as you do not have an easy comparison.

I found out first hand how difficult it is to determine a fair sales price when working with the Purchase Tax Authorities in the UK and the Upper Finance Authority in Germany and the Custom Authorities in many countries. We were only leasing machinery and not selling the machinery anywhere in the world so there was no recognized sales price to compare.

The Japanese understand very well the difficulty in establishing a price (if you have no direct comparison) and they may keep on dumping if they don't get caught. And it's hard to prove in most cases.

12) Another area in which business and government should work together is to stop the give away of some high tech industries especially when they face trouble. Japan does this regularly even with low tech. For example, when **Subaru** of America (the distributor) got in trouble, Fuji bailed them out. When Daihatsu got in trouble, Toyota bailed them out. We have seen a number of such actions by the Japanese these past few years. Fortunately, IBM came to the rescue of the chip machinery manufacturing division of Perkins Elmer to keep it from falling into foreign hands. That was our last chip machinery manufacturer in America.

Unfortunately, many others have slipped away. Even though government pressure stopped the sale of Fairchild Semiconductor Corporation to Fujitsu, Fairchild entered into a cooperative arrangement that may not be much different in the real world.

The easy licensing of American technology over the past 30 years has come back to haunt many American companies. The list is long and very sad. The harm that this has brought to America is very great. On the other hand, if companies hadn't licensed the technology, the Japanese companies may have just helped themselves, free of charge, as they did to the basic chip patent of Texas Instruments.

The past few years when I have been working with many American companies to penetrate the China market, I have seen a new attitude. The most important and key point on the minds of every one of my clients was, **I don't want to develop another competitor.** It was good to hear this real concern of American manufacturers. We are waking up.

Fortunately, protecting high technology usually was not a big problem in China since intitially they were in no shape to use the latest technology even though they thought they were.

Another key point when there is a concern that you may be developing a new competitor in some of your markets is to restrict the markets that your licensee can sell to. But enough. That is the subject of a whole other book.

13) We are seeing more and more companies waking up to our problems of manufacturing good products in America.

We see the Saturn Motor Company of General Motors starting from scratch to make a complete new car in a new plant to shake off the past. While they have a way to go, the car I drove was great. It is a step in the right direction. We, however, do see the influence of Japanese brainwashing on the media when writing test reports on the Saturn and its three Japanese competitors. My impression of the article in one auto magazine was that the biggest problem with the Saturn was that it was noisier than the Japanese cars. But when I studied the test data in the report, it was only two to three decibels noisier at idle and the same to one decibel more at highway speed. Noisier! I challenge you to detect that with your ears. And besides, the Saturn has a more powerful engine.

The most surprising part of the test in my mind relates to safety. The Saturn stopped more quickly with its regular brakes than the **Nissan Sentra** did with **anti-lock brakes.**

Very little comment was made on the high tech plastic body panels on the Saturn. I just learned that a new expensive BMW model will also have plastic body panels. Not bad company.

Then we have those wonderful long range thinking

people in Congress who passed a law that forbids US companies from including their imported cars in the domestic fuel efficiency calculations. But the law gave strange results. The cars made at the GM/Toyota Joint Venture in California can't count in the GM fuel efficiency calculations as they have less than 75% US content. However Toyota as a foreign manufacturer can count them in their calculations. The second surprise is that now US manufacturers make sure more than 25% of the parts of their gas guzzlers are made overseas so they are excluded from the companies minimum mileage calculation. So the American manufacturers get hurt and we help the foreign manufacturers.

Other companies are waking up also. The advertisement by Dreyfus Securities in the May 9, 1990, *Wall Street Journal* really gets to the point. The headline in the ad below a number of photos of American buildings, land, farms, hotels, and resorts that had been purchased by foreign investors said, "Teach Your Children to Save or Teach Them a Foreign Language." Dreyfus was calling our attention to the fact that we are poor savers. Without our savings, corporations can't borrow the money to modernize or build new plants.

Once we save we then only have to get the banks to loan the money to sound manufacturing ventures and not to wild developers, buyout experts or our other countries which caused so much trouble in the 80's. A mistake that we taxpayers will be paying for for many years.

Let's wake up, America, and move forward. □

Section IV:

The Difficult, But Simple Solutions All Americans Can Take Part In

AS WE REVIEW *the various solutions for America to shake off its Colonial Master—Japan—we realize we have few options. Years ago we could have solved the problem quite easily but as time has passed we have lost more and more control of our destiny. As I see it we cannot expect much help from our government. It has been ineffective for the last 15 years as our trade deficit has kept increasing.*

We have finally seen some good progress by producers as they recognize the demands for quality, service and penetration of international markets. But the American companies hands are often tied because of their fear of retaliation by the Japanese, if they speak out against Japanese trade practices.

*The only real sure and quick solution is for **"We The People"** to take matters into our own hands. We must take this action* **NOW**,

TO PROTECT OUR JOBS,
OUR CHILDRENS FUTURE AND
OUR STANDARD OF LIVING.

THE CHOICE IS OURS!!

Chapter 14:

WHAT THE GOVERNMENT CAN DO—IF WE FORCE IT TO

I'VE TRIED TO devise a group of solutions that "kill two (or more) birds with one stone" in trying to get at some of our most intractable national problems. I begin with six suggestions. The aim of these suggestions is to reduce dependence on imports and the related trade deficit problem. To protect the environment in several ways. To reduce domestic government spending and thereby reduce the budget deficit.

1) **Become more self-sufficient in energy** and depend more on our immediate neighbors, Mexico and Canada, for the oil and gas we cannot produce. This can cut the dependence on politically dangerous middle-eastern countries and help solidify our regional neighbors, helping them prosper and expand our most natural export markets. Also, this can reduce the environmental hazards of so much ocean-going tanker imported oil. I understand there is far less environmental risk to producing oil in many of the restricted areas of America than there is in thousands of oil tankers coming to our shores.

    Increasing the gas tax by .50 to $1.00 per gallon with a rebate for the poor and those who commute long distances to work is a part of this solution. This tax should be used to maintain our infrastructure for greater economic growth. This will also reduce imports and the chances for environmental disasters that come with supertankers importing oil.

2) **All oil imported to America must be in double bottom tankers.** If not in double bottom ships an environmental

fee of $5.00 per barrel will be collected by the Government from the importer and 80% used to reduce deficit, 20% to cover spills, etc.

These first two suggestions will reduce spills, reduce consumption, reduce the trade deficit, reduce the budget deficit, reduce air pollution, increase savings, and increase domestic oil exploration.

3) **Keep the dollar weak to encourage exports and discourage imports.** This may be difficult but some countries seem to know how to keep their currencies under valued to help exports.

4) **All parts imported for assembly at transplant ("screwdriver") assembly plants, of which the final product is not at least 75% American content, will be subject to an inspection fee of 20% of the value of the part.**

5) **Until Japan permits American companies to sell any legal product in Japan directly or otherwise without restriction (such as meat, rice, lumber products, cigarettes, spirits, and cars) there will be an inspection—distribution rights fee of 15% on all imported Japanese products.**

Each time I have suggested to Japanese officials that I was considering setting up a supermarket in Japan when I retired and sell rice, meat, wine, cigarettes, citrus fruits, etc., they became very upset and said I wouldn't be allowed to do that as those items were forbidden or restricted imports. They made it quite clear they had a right to do that but we couldn't restrict their imports to America as it would violate GATT rules. Apparently, Japan has some divine right to live by a different set of rules but not America. And we are suckers enough to let them get away with it.

6) **Don't build any more prisons. To further reduce our deficit—use surplus military bases (and we have a sur-**

plus) for all nonviolent criminals.

Maintain the same standards at the bases for the prisoners as we do for our soldiers. (Except no weekend passes.)

Have the prisoners do the work of maintaining the bases as our soldiers now do and maybe more. They also can be trained to rehabilitate more barracks if more are needed. This will cost only a fraction of the $168 per day it costs New York City to keep a prisoner at Rikers Island.

A key group of prisoners for this project would be **drug users** and **low level drug pushers** but in separate prisons. The facilities at most military bases are quite adequate for training the prisoners for a new way of life.

I realize that the accommodations at our military bases will not be as fancy as some of our traditional prisons but if they are good enough for our soldiers, they are too good for the convicts.

Make all the prisoners pay for their stay at these rehabilitation bases either from their ill gotten gains or future earnings after they are released.

A lot of concertina wire and barbed wire can be put around the facilities to be sure the prisoners don't stray away. But even if a few do escape, it's better than having thousands of criminals walking our streets because we don't have prison space or sentences are too short. This action should save our country much money and at the same time make it safer.

In the following pages of this Chapter, I will outline some suggestions on how we can copy Japanese policies **exactly** and use **reciprocity** to achieve a level playing field.

Our government must realize it's dealing with the Japanese from a position of **strength,** not **weakness.**

The Government must also realize that Japan is a great economic power because its trade and dealings with America made it that way. But this economic strength was realized almost entirely because we have given them free access to our market and they have restricted us from theirs. This increased our costs and made us less competitive in the world markets. Much of the economic power of Japan would collapse very quickly if we put the same restrictions on our markets as they do on theirs. And they realize this. That's why they fight so hard to keep us out and America open. They are working rapidly to entrench themselves in our markets before we wake up.

I would suggest our government take a **strong stand** and advise Japan we are going to start playing the game by **their rules.**

For example, if they have a 20% duty on Plywood for some alleged reason, we copy them **exactly** and put a 20% duty on say VCRs. We will keep the 20% duty on VCRs for the **same period** of time that they **have kept the 20% duty on plywood.** If they have had that duty on for four years and it takes them another year to remove it (due to foot dragging), we will keep the duty on VCRs for a total of **five years.**

If they have prohibited rice imports for say 20 years since we first asked them to open up that market and they still keep it for another two years, we advise then that we will put an **exact duplicate restriction** on **Japanese computers** for 20 years plus the two years it takes them to open up the rice market. Once they know we are serious (like Reagan was with Kadaffi—Bush with Saddam) we will start to have some serious trade negotiations. Of course, the trade negotiators who have to carry out this work will not have a chance to get a high paying job with the Japanese when they leave their government job.

Another example of **copying them exactly** is found in the experience I related when we couldn't get their approval to bring in baseball bats unless they were inspected upon arrival in Japan. We suggested to MITI we would follow the Japanese example and start inspecting their products upon arrival in the U.S.A. I jokingly suggested that was a good idea and maybe we should start inspecting their cars after they arrived. From their reaction I concluded they felt they had some special right to inspect products after arrival in Japan but we in America did not have that right.

We hear a lot of talk in America about how our consumers will suffer if we put the same restrictions on imports as other countries put on us. I'm talking mainly about **consumer items** where such impact can be more easily noted.

Yet, you rarely hear anyone saying how the poor Japanese consumer suffers because of their restrictions. For example, a fine steak that we can buy here for $3 to $4 per pound costs $20 to $30 per pound in Japan. And this similarity applies to many products.

Yet, the Japanese survive quite well. They save more. Don't eat as much beef. Buy up Rockefeller Center and Columbia Pictures and MCA and sell us a lot of consumer goods so we don't save much, eat too much, and virtually become a captured colony of Japan.

Some people say that even if they could buy beef at fair prices they wouldn't do it. But those people are badly misinformed. Mr. Davis who testified with me before Senator Heinz on Japan trade problems told some interesting stories.

Some years ago the U.S. Government stocked a ship with many U.S.A. products and toured the Asian ports to show what America could offer. It was called "Boatique America."

One of the items offered for sale was **beef.** When the Japanese heard there was beef on the ship and it would be sold to Japanese consumers who visited the ship, strange things started to happen.

Let me quote from the record of the hearings on **Barriers to Foreign Trade** before the U.S. Senate SubCommittee on International Finance and Monetary Policy, Chaired by Senator Heinz. Quote Mr. Davis:

"when we had this boatique American—this 130 metric tons of beef—the Japanese unions first told the Department of Commerce they were going to picket the ship if U.S. beef was carried on board. I immediately went to the United Food and Commercial Workers and the Seafarers International Unions who sent off telegrams and said the minute you put a picket on there we're going to picket the first ship that comes in with Japanese automobiles and you won't get one automobile in. The next day we were told the Japanese were told not to picket our ship. That's the kind of thing they understand."

As you can see, you have to play "hardball" with Japan.

And the Japanese understand very well. Regarding the myth that the Japanese consumer isn't interested in buying American products, Mr. Davis went on to say at the hearings:

"Japan's 'lack of demand' issue is sheer nonsense. Three Japanese meat promotions stand out in my mind; the Harumi International food show, Kansai Cold Stores food show (Osaka) and the Boatique America show. At the Harumi show, 30 metric tons of mostly Portion Control meats were exhibited and completely sold out in less than four hours. The Kansai show had approximately 20 metric tons of Portion Control meats which were sold out so quickly that they had to be rationed, and police were called in to help quell the unruly crowds trying to obtain U.S. beef products.

"Boatique America is the most significant example, where 130 metric tons (out of 1,000 metric tons requested by the U.S. Department of Commerce) were completely sold out. Sales were described by the press as follows: 'America's latest effort to promote exports to Japan—a floating department store—proved at least one thing during five days of sales here.'

"Japanese consumers like American beef, or at least they like the prices.

"By the time the 13,082-ton Shin Sakura-Maru left Tokyo Wednesday to move to the second of 13 ports of call in Japan, beef sales had accounted for almost 24 percent of the $646,702 worth of merchandise sold aboard the ship which was anchored at Harumi Pier. The next best-selling category-women's apparel-brought in only about half as much.

"The crowds, especially over the weekend, were large and many people went directly to the beef counter on the lower deck where sirloin was selling for $7.59 a pound-a bargain by Japanese standards. Weekend crowds were so big that thousands had to be turned away.

"Beef sales, which were restricted to 2.2 pounds (one kilogram) per customer, were cut off after four hours one day when the daily allocation of 2,600 kilograms (5,720 pounds) ran out."

Senator Heinz:

"Is that why Australia has a higher percentage of the market? Are we being discriminated against because we are trying to get in there and the Australians—"

Mr. Davis:

"The Australians play hardball. That's reciprocity to them. The Australians say, 'If you don't buy our bauxite, we won't sell you our meat, and if you don't buy so much meat, we won't sell you the bauxite.' They look at items the Japanese must have and they indicate to them that unless they buy meat, unless they buy a lot of meat, they won't sell them bauxite, which is necessary in Japan. The Australians are not afraid to intimidate the Japanese, which is exactly what the Japanese do with most other people.

"During the calendar 1980, Japan imported a total of 121,889 metric tons of meat, beef broken down as follows: Australia, 92,935 metric tons (76.2 percent); the United States, 22,437 metric tons (18.4 percent); and other countries, 6,517 metric tons (5.3 percent). It must be mentioned that U.S. meat is federally inspected, while Australian, and that of most other countries, is not. Additionally, the U.S. provides grain-fed cattle, while Australia's cattle are grass-fed, resulting in meat of a lower quality."

To appreciate how rough the Japanese are at intimidating American companies, Senator Heinz made this statement to all of us who were testifying before him. Senator Heinz:

"We invited a very substantial number of other industry groups and individuals to testify at this hearing or to submit statements for the record. Many of them declined and **gave oblique reference to their fear that they would be retaliated against by the Japanese Government,** and I at first want to congratulate the present witnesses for their courage in being here.

"Second, I want it on the record that if there is any retaliation against any of the witnesses or their industry groups or any of the companies associated with those industry groups, if there's any hint of retaliation by the Japanese for Americans coming forward before a congressional committee and speaking their minds, then the Japanese Government will find out what retaliation is all about, because we will not stand idly by if that kind of fear tactic is pursued. I hope the fears expressed by the witnesses who didn't come, who declined to come, are groundless. I hope that a great country like Japan would never for a minute consider such a tactic, but in the event there is in some bureaucracies some place such an instinct, I want it clearly understood what the consequences would be, and they would be grave, they would be immediate, and they would be unanimous."

These facts destroy the myth that the Japanese people wouldn't buy our products if they were available. They destroy the myth that the Japanese don't buy our products because of poor quality. Yet, when they import beef, it's mainly the lower quality beef that they import not our high quality product.

You soon realize that many of the Japanese statements are propaganda, not facts.

The American people never had a chance to hear of our trade problems with Japan as no American media, to our knowledge, was at the hearings.

But the Japanese considered these hearings very important. The Committee room was filled with a large Japanese television crew, Japanese reporters and Japanese lobbyists.

Later, the Japanese newspapers published our pictures and comments about us in their newspapers. I guess we were one of their original "Gangs of four."

But you can see, in spite of the outstanding efforts of people like Senator Heinz, our government does very little to really address our trade problems.

As one businessman stated: "Our trade representatives don't go to Japan to negotiate, they just compromise!"

Until our government gets some courage and backbone and learns how to negotiate, very little progress will be made. They need to learn how to use some strong words and actions with Japan—engaging in reciprocity, playing hardball, public embarrassment and copying Japanese trade barriers **exactly.**

But if they do, they have little hope of becoming a highly paid Japanese lobbyist or agent.

Here are a few specific actions our government could take that would get the Japanese government's attention and hence lead to some meaningful negotiations.

While I have little hope that our Government—the Administration or Congress, has the will or the courage to do this and see that the American people and the Japanese consumers are treated fairly, I will still propose a plan. **Require Japan to play fair**—Copy their barriers **exactly** and use **reciprocity** to enforce.

EXAMPLES:

Current Japan Action	Proposed USA Action
1) Bans import of rice	Ban Japanese computers
2) 20% duty on plywood	20% duty on Japanese textiles
3) Limits US beef to about 60,000 tons	Limit import of Japanese FAX machines to 60,000 with same duties they charge on beef
4) Limits on US cigarettes advertising and distribution	Place similar limits on Japanese Video games
5) Limits US Department stores in Japan	Place similar limits on Japanese establishing auto parts manufacturing companies in America
6) Limits US law firms use of name, etc.	Place same limits on Japanese Financial firms

The key is to try to copy the Japanese restriction **exactly.** If it's alright for Japan, it must be alright for us to do the same. This would not only greatly improve the situation of the American worker and farmer but it would be a great gift to the Japanese consumer. The Japanese would no longer have to pay $20 to $30 a pound for beef that we can buy for $3 or $4 a pound.

They could buy rice for a fraction of their present cost.

Prices on many items in Japanese department stores would drop 10% to 50% or more.

The Japanese Auto Transplants would have to buy parts from American parts manufacturers, instead of Japanese parts manufacturers coming to America, unless they open their markets.

When the Japanese government or its hirelings complain we can call them "American Bashers."

You may think some of these ideas are "far out," ridiculous and rough but I learned them from observing and working with the Japanese. They are great teachers!! □

Chapter 15:

WHAT BUSINESSES CAN DO

THERE ARE MANY things that our businesses (including manufacturing, banking, farming, services, etc.) can do to make us more competitive in the world markets and at home. There are a few key items that should be implemented as soon as possible before we lose more control over our future.

SAVINGS RATE

First, the people in America should **increase their savings rate. Business must develop incentive plans, bonus plans and retirement plans for all workers, that encourage savings and at the same time improve productivity and quality. Examples of such plans are discussed below.** We are **big consumers** but very **poor savers** compared to Japan and most of the developed world. The explanation for this is that we are a wasteful society, we are too involved with keeping up with the "Jones's", we have little discipline, we live for today and hope tomorrow will be OK.

Of course it would be helpful if banks stopped sending out pre-approved credit cards.

Unfortunately, most of the solutions to this savings problem that have been proposed in the past have been made by economists and financial experts. I would not really call them solutions but comments on our savings problem.

While all their insights have been most interesting and helpful, they have failed to bring into the picture the human behavior aspect which is probably the most important factor of all in achieving the desired results.

Having lived in Japan and worked with the Japanese for so

many years, I have admired their very simple solution to this problem. While it is true they have a very disciplined and nationalistic society, and when the word comes down, you do this or you do that and it is not questioned, it is easier to achieve certain goals. Also without social security as we know it they have a real incentive to save. As you may know even key executives in large corporations, if they don't become the chairman or president, are put out to pasture at the age of about 55. This all leads to a real incentive to save.

All workers at all levels are paid a basic monthly wage. Then in June and in December they are normally paid an extra month's pay for a total of 14 months. If the company does quite well, they are paid two month's extra in each June and December. In fact, when our Joint Venture in Japan was doing very well, we paid four month's extra in both June and December for a total of 20 month's pay. The wonderfully wise Japanese wife then puts most of this extra found money in a savings account since they had lived quite well on the basic monthly pay. And you wonder why the Japanese save a large portion of their wages! And you wonder why our Japanese workers produced so many high quality products and made our company so successful!!

At the same time, the workers work very hard since they know that if the company does well they will get a large bonus. They also know that if they do not make quality products that can be sold, they will miss their bonus.

Over the years we tried incentive plans for as many of our workers as I could in our operations around the world and we found similar results. We did have a little difficulty with the corporate management board who made us reduce the top limit on a bonus from 50% to 35% of their salary. They also got quite concerned when we included the Manager of International Credit and Collections and the Manager of International Traffic and Shipping in the incentive plan. But the results were excellent—when we doubled our export business in two years, the accounts receivable remained at the same level in spite of doubling the sales.

Fortunately, we do have some companies in the U.S.A. who do try to follow similar plans. But I note, much to my surprise, it is often fought by the labor unions, as in the case of Boeing and is not encouraged by our government. The arguments in the Boeing case were that if you get part of your pay as a bonus, it does not get calculated as a part of your base pay and it affects your pension, etc. But that is not a real argument as it can be resolved quite easily. We simply added it to the base pay for pension purposes.

Another argument is that many managers don't want the workers to share in the good results, they want to save it all for themselves as if they were totally responsible for any good results. At the same time the unions do not like the idea because if the workers do a good job and reach high productivity goals, make high quality products and get a big bonus, the union can't claim that it did a lot for the worker. Some day we will get smart like the Japanese and learn what makes things work.

You may think this would not work in the U.S.A. but I disagree. While governments are different and policies may differ, fundamentally **people are very much alike.**

Probably one of the biggest benefits of an incentive pay system is the high productivity and the quality of work it delivers. The bonuses are based on performance so not only do the people have this nice lump sum to put away in the bank but it does not come unless every one in the company has performed very well. So it is a great incentive to do high quality work, to work hard, to be dedicated and not to waste. All of this would be a great plus and make America competitive in the market place and at the same time improve our savings.

While not a direct incentive plan, probably one of the best solid long range savings plan is the plan introduced in 1991 by IBM. Although they refer to it as a retirement plan it really gets everyone saving early in life. As I understand the plan a portion of an employee's annual salary increases will be put in this special savings plan and the balance of the increase paid to the employee in the regular manner. Apparently to stop any criticism of this forced savings IBM put in 5% of the 1991 salary to start the plan operating. None of this can be taken by the employee until they retire.

The government also can help the American people save. We had a good program of IRA's that was most successful in improving our savings. But then the government started spending so much money that our congressmen needed more taxes to pay for all kinds of things, many of which we could do without, so they taxed all of our savings.

LONG TERM THINKING

Our problem goes back to this American's desire to have everything now. In Japan, they think a little **longer term,** and are not pressured by our Wall Street geniuses who only look at the results very **short term.** Must have a good quarter! Unfortunately, they are not doing very well as the Japanese keep buying them up or push them aside.

I still remember very well the year our group had a great success in our Joint Venture in Japan and we had more sales and profits than anyone could believe was possible. Many of my fellow executives would comment about the good results and how quickly our group had grown. They thought this had all happened over 2 or 3 years. They didn't realize we had been working on that project for 13 years! Most good results don't come quickly.

The average American businessman and Wall Street experts do not realize what is happening as the Japanese take that long term look at the market. They don't mind struggling for a few years as long as there is a pot of gold at the end which, in their terms, is the domination of a market. They are particularly happy if it is the domination of the American market so they can live on easy street the rest of their lives.

We see too many American companies buying back their stock so they look better to Wall Street. The share price goes up and Wall Street loves it, but the competitive core of the business is not strengthened.

Usually that money could have been spent much more wisely in buying more new modern production machinery, spending more on developing new products and improving existing products.

We see companies repurchase large amounts of their stocks instead of spending it on new products. Possibly they just don't have any ideas on how to spend the money on research or new product development.

MANUFACTURING ECONOMY

We must change our goals and drive to develop a **manufacturing** economy, not a **service** economy. In the 1980's, we heard all the great thoughts on how we should become a service economy. That's nice clean easy work. We move money around, we sell fast food, etc. But we don't create anything. All it did was do away with high paying manufacturing jobs and place people in low paying service jobs. Of course, the Japanese invasion of our markets, due in part to our neglect, accelerated this process.

CAPITAL

We misuse the capital we have. We keep hearing the stories that we don't have enough capital to modernize our industries due to our low savings rate. That is certainly true to some degree but we have even bigger problems. We misuse the capital we have.

We apparently had a surplus of capital but it was wasted in the 1980's. You only have to look at the billions of dollars in bad loans made to other nations. Then you look at the hundreds of billions of bad loans by various banks and financial institutions to property developers and leveraged buyouts. This was a case of those people getting too greedy and trying to make big profits on risky loans only to end up with massive losses.

That money could have been used much better if businesses would have had the common sense and courage to borrow the money to improve their manufacturing and the greedy bankers would have loaned the money to improve our country instead of destroying it.

The banks thought they were going to get 12 to 15% on their risky loans but ended up after write offs with large negative returns.

RETALIATION

We must retaliate against Japan when they retaliate against us. American companies that have operations in Japan find it most difficult to directly press the Japanese for the fear of retaliation. As noted in Chapter 14, Senator Heinz pointed out that when he invited companies to testify on trade barriers, many refused to do that for fear of retaliation by Japan. This is a serious problem that the Japanese will deny but which businesses know is very real. I have had the same experience when I have contacted companies while writing this book. Even companies who have been badly hurt by the Japanese, companies who have had their patents effectively stolen will not talk about their problems, apparently for fear of retaliation in some other area.

MARKET PENETRATION

Business must penetrate all markets including the closed markets of Japan, China and Korea.

We can't let other countries dominate more and more of the new developing markets of the world. American businesses and government need to work diligently to help set up, then foster, and finally sell into new market-based systems in Eastern

Europe and China. It can be done. In the four years that we worked intensively selling AMF products into China, China became AMF's 5th largest market in the world. I firmly believe that America has a natural advantage over the Japanese in working with both the Eastern Europeans and the Chinese—if we try!!

American companies must keep pressing our government to demand that Japan and other countries open their markets so that Japanese and other consumers and manufacturers have access to our goods like we have access to theirs.

SOURCING

Business must try to buy more of their materials and goods in America. This is an area where businesses can make a great step to improve our economy at once. This will take a lot of effort on the part of all Americans but it can be done. In fact, it is already happening with some retailers with real courage. It can also happen with many more retailers and manufacturers if they really understand the possible end results and benefits. We have seen the excellent work done in this area by Wal-Mart stores. Here is the biggest and probably most successful retailer in America which has a strong policy to buy American goods whenever possible. They appreciate that their customers and hence their success comes from the working people of America.

If WalMart buys all of its goods overseas to save a few percent, those American customers will have fewer good paying jobs and buy less at WalMart.

Unfortunately, we are bombarded with propaganda that if we import less or restrict imports to some degree, the cost of products in America will rise. While that may have a thread of truth, it completely ignores the more important side of the equation which is you first have to earn money before you spend it. If you don't have a job or a good paying job, it doesn't really matter if that pair of imported pants cost $12 against American made pants costing $15.

We see this argument made many times when some restriction is suggested on automobiles. All the Japanese car dealers make a big noise about how many of the people working at their dealership will be let out of work. They completely overlook the hundreds of thousands of American workers out of work not only at our auto manufacturing plants but in the hundreds of industries that support our auto industry. And the Japanese transplant factories that are coming to America don't help much since most of the key parts are made overseas. That means all of the higher paying jobs are not in America.

And those Americans who lost their skilled jobs had to take service jobs that pay only a fraction of what they earned before.

Even though the retailers can do a lot to help, other businesses can do even more. The guideline is, wherever possible, buy raw material and components that will directly or indirectly add more good paying American jobs. This can take many forms. Maybe it's the textile that goes in a manufacturer's clothing or upholstery. Even if some of the assembly, for some reason may be in an overseas plant, at least the materials that go into the product can be manufactured in America. When companies buy fork lift trucks, or other machinery, try to buy in America even if it may be slightly more expensive. The workers at those plants will then be in a position to buy your products. The chances that the workers in foreign plants will buy your products are most remote.

A recent example of where an American company is buying overseas and taking thousands of jobs from American workers is the recent action by Federal Express. They announced in July 1991 they are buying 70 airbus A-300 Aircraft from France. They of course are free to buy from whomever they want and we, the consumers and businesses in America, are free not to use Federal Express services. Federal Express may well find that if enough of us use other services like UPS, who for example use American Aircraft, they may not need those 70 A-300 Aircraft. I fully appreciate Federal Express may want to buy some French Aircraft since they also service the European market and that is quite proper. But we the American people and American businesses should not support Federal if they don't support us.

GO GLOBAL

Don't be embarrassed if sometimes you must put your manufacturing plant overseas to be able to penetrate the local market. Many times that is due to high duties or protected markets.

In fact, in many countries, such as Japan, they may not even let your product in the country or if they do it gets so marked up in the distribution system it will not sell.

In the forty some years that I was involved in international business, we had to put manufacturing plants in such countries as the UK. First we did so to serve the EFTA (European Free Trade Association), and later, when the United Kingdom joined the Common Market to serve that.

But in every case where the plants were set up in UK, Japan, China, Australia, and so forth to penetrate those markets, our exports to those countries **increased very substantially.** And we, like the Japanese today, shipped most of the higher tech critical parts from our factories in America to be put in the products.

GOOD MANUFACTURING JOBS

We can and must become a strong manufacturing economy.

If we just keep in mind that our American people cannot continue buying products made in America unless we give them a good job, the picture becomes quite clear.

We also must remember that, when we have all the problems of welfare, budget deficits, crime and so forth in our cities, it is primarily because we have lost our manufacturing industries

You see this so clearly when a city like Bridgeport, Connecticut, goes into bankruptcy. Not many years ago, Bridgeport was the brass manufacturing capital of the world. So with no good jobs, people are not able to pay taxes or buy products and services in the city, we have great problems.

We see in June 1991, Japan's trade surplus reached its highest level in three years. Our trade deficit declined ever so slightly because of our recession. In fact, business was so bad, people couldn't even buy Japanese products.

If American manufacturers want to create jobs and make products the American people will buy they must do a number of things:

1) Listen to the employees, they have many good ideas.

2) Listen to customers—Learn what they want

3) Remember you must make a **quality** product and **service** it.

4) Sell world wide at fair prices—don't get too greedy. Forty percent of nothing is nothing.

5) Control run away top Executive compensation. This not only makes you non-competitive but it demoralizes the workers and angers the American public.

6) Have the courage and foresight to modernize your factories.

7) Don't be greedy—Control not only costs, but prices.

8) Change incentives for management and employees. Pay bonuses to improve quality, productivity and savings.

Hopefully, some day soon, if we take the correct bold actions, the trade imbalance with Japan will drop even more—not because of a recession—but because we are buying American goods made in booming American factories.

Wake up America before it's too late. □

Chapter 16:

WHAT WE THE PEOPLE CAN DO

I SEE VERY little hope that we can expect much help from our government to solve these trade problems. Based on it's track record over the past few years we have made very little progress. This is particularly true with regard to Japan.

On the surface, it may look like our trade imbalance with Japan has improved a few billion dollars. It really isn't true. Japan has simply switched the source of its' exports from Japan to several other Southeast Asian countries. You see Sony radios coming from Korea, refrigerator compressors from Singapore, most of the Japanese power train in Hyundai Autos coming via Korea. There are also various Japanese companies exports to the USA coming from Thailand and Korea and other areas. If these are all added in to the imports we get directly from Japan our trade imbalance may actually have increased.

We can't expect much help from our producers for the various reasons noted in Chapter 15. However, we are seeing a great renewed effort by our manufacturers to make top quality products and to export more. The weak dollar has done wonders to help our overall trade imbalance.

So it really ends up that "We the People" must solve the problem. Fortunately, we don't have all the problems of government or business when they are criticized by foreign governments or businesses. So with this great power and freedom we should act **aggressively** but **quietly**.

The first thing is for the majority of the American people to understand the problem and the solution.

Before we suggest what we should do, we must first understand the real problem facing America. It seems that we are bombarded daily by the financial experts and economists, who suggest the only way America can work its way out of the recession is for the consumers to start spending. They point out that two thirds of the spending is by consumers and only one third by business and government.

What they **fail to point** out is **how the consumer should spend.** If the spending is on new housing that would be good as almost all of the materials and labor in housing are sourced in America. That creates American jobs.

You may think that the above statement contradicts the section on increasing our savings in Chapter 15. It is quite true that if the consumer spends money on products that don't increase the income of the American worker that will reduce our savings.

But if the money is spent on products that are made in America, American workers have more income so they can buy the product and still have something left over to increase the overall savings.

However, if that spending is on imported automobiles, electronic equipment, etc., it has very little effect on helping America out of a recession. The money you pay for that imported product goes overseas to pay for their workers, for their materials, overhead and profit. We get only a few service jobs in America from that product. The spending on those imported goods not only doesn't generate any good jobs in America but it reduces our savings and increases our trade and budget deficits. It generates very little taxable earnings in America.

It is quite clear that spending on domestic manufactured products has several times the good impact on our economy as spending on imported products.

We have to recognize the overall effect of buying a domestic manufactured product—not only for the manufacturer and its workers, but for their suppliers and the suppliers' suppliers, etc.

Also, the impact on all the local businesses near the factory, from the barber or hairdresser to the carpenter or plumber, to the local clothing store, to the doctor or dentist, must be added in. These local businesses are all supported by the American worker. It is quite true that when foreign consumers buy our products they are also supporting the American worker, unfortunately not many foreign consumers are or can buy our products.

When American working people have good jobs, particularly in manufacturing:

1) They pay taxes in America.
2) They are not on welfare.
3) They do not collect unemployment insurance.
4) They have money to spend in America.

When they don't have good manufacturing jobs, we get the reverse situation. This is a prime cause of many of the troubles our cities and states are facing. We see Bridgeport, Connecticut, go into bankruptcy because they collect too few taxes and have such a burden to support the unemployed. We see similar problems in New York City and Philadelphia. Of course, all of those people added to the government payroll only compounded the problem.

I have noticed that Japanese, German and Korean workers who made so many of those products we buy, don't spend much money in America or pay taxes in America. I couldn't help but smile to myself when I read the headline in the *New York Times* on June, 20, 1991, "Trade Gap Widened in April. **Deficit is Viewed as Sign of Recovery."** It goes on to quote the experts supporting this viewpoint.

My comment is—forgive them dear Lord for they know not what they say! None of those increased imports **added jobs in America.** It probably only means the people had enough confidence to go deeper into debt. Now the increase in **exports** in April was positive—that added jobs in America.

This all goes to explain why our standard of living in America keeps going down and down. Yet, for some strange reason, rarely does anyone look at the real cause of the problem—**lack of manufacturing in America and people to buy American products.** Possibly the solution is so simple it gets overlooked.

Besides, a politician can make very little "political hay" supporting this solution, compared to criticizing his political opponents for their bad solutions to our problems.

As was noted earlier in the book, the big problems with the deficits, both budget and trade, and the troubles in our cities didn't start with the current 1990-91 recession. These problems started long ago. The recession only accented them.

The loss of our American manufacturing base and the restrictions on selling to many countries has been developing for years. The strong dollar in the past has only made the problems worse. We can also see the problems this lack of manufacturing in America is causing for our young people.

The 1991 class of college graduates is having a most difficult time finding jobs. In fact, it is almost impossible to even get an interview.

The first reaction of many people is that this is because we are in a recession. The economic experts say the only way out of the recession is for the consumers to spend more. But in March 1991, our income went up 0.2% and our spending went up 0.6%. Yet, we fell deeper into a recession.

The consumers can't spend more since they are already spending faster than their income is increasing. The savings rate is at a new low. In fact, in March, people had to get more credit or dip into savings to make up the 0.4% shortfall.

The solution is not simply spending more but on where you spend your money.

You can see there is a much deeper cause for the lack of new jobs for our graduates than the current recession. It is the loss of our manufacturing base over the past several years. Our trading partners probably understand this quite well.

The real problem is that our spending is going to buy imported products—not products made in America. The money has gone overseas. Therefore, our manufacturers don't need to hire more people. (In fact, they are laying off people).

The graduates should not be surprised at this shortage of good jobs, nor should their professors or guidance counselors be surprised. All they have to do is look in the parking lot and see all the Japanese cars, or other foreign cars, or look in their rooms and see the Japanese computers, VCRs, and other products.

You soon realize that this has resulted in a reduction in sales of American products. When General Motors sales go down, Ford sales go down, Chrysler sales go down, IBM sales go down, you have a problem. In such a downturn these companies don't need to hire many new graduates—particularly when they have to lay off other workers. To compound the problem, when General Motors sales drop, they don't need steel from U.S. Steel. They don't need plastics from DuPont or General Electric. They don't need tires from Goodyear. They don't need glass from Libby Owens and Ford, and so forth. This means that all these companies and many more need fewer and fewer new employees.

Then it goes down to the next echelon. When U.S. Steel (USX) doesn't ship steel, they don't need to buy ore from the mining companies, or coke from the coal companies, and so on.

As you look at this problem from afar and with a little bit of common sense, you soon realize that until we start buying more products made in our country by our manufacturers the future is going to be very dim.

It is true some of the foreign companies who make or assemble products in America help out some, depending on the local content. The "screwdriver" plants (which only assemble imported parts) are not much help.

If it is more important for the graduate or student to still buy that imported product, then they have another course of action.

My suggestion is that they learn Japanese. Then they may have an opportunity to possibly get a job with a Japanese company which may have a transplant factory in America. It will not be a high level job—just a job. But with the Japanese language ability they may someday rise to a middle level job. But rest assured the Japanese will never permit a "Gaijin" (a foreigner) to hold one of the top positions. We Americans routinely made local nationals the heads of our foreign subsidiaries. In fact, when I was with AMF, we made Mr. Nishikata, President of our Japanese subsidiary AMF-KK and we made Mr. Itoh, (the Chairman of C. Itoh) a member of the board of directors of our parent company. Poor T. Boone Pinkens who was the largest stockholder in a Japanese company could not even get himself on that board.

So while working for a Japanese company may be an option I do not think the future is what the graduate might have hope for.

The great thing about this is that we live in a free country. The choice is ours. It isn't up to the Japanese. It isn't up to GM or GE to determine what our future will be. It's in our own hands. I wouldn't want to suggest that "We the People" are the root of all our problems. Our government has been very weak in trade deals. Our manufacturers and the workers have made some sloppy products, our unions have saddled us with costly and outdated work rules, all of which pushed us to consider imports. But that is changing very fast.

Having spent most of my life selling American products around the world, I am a firm believer in foreign trade but it must be **fair**. Not **free** trade but **fair** trade, as was said by a famous union leader some years ago. We do not have **fair** trade today.

If our new graduates understood this situation and their families who sacrificed so much to send them to school did also, and they decided to buy American products in the future, the impact would be felt at once by our trading partners and our U.S. manufacturers.

If similar actions were taken also by our minorities who have been so criticized by the Japanese, by the people who are upset with the Japanese trade support for the Apartheid government of South Africa, and the women who really believe in the rights of women, the impact would be great.

The Japanese could not criticize our government and businesses since they would not have been involved. The only people who could be criticized would be "We the People." We who have bought so many foreign goods and made the foreign suppliers so profitable and strong.

The choice is ours. Do you want a good job in the future or will you be happy with the bleak alternatives of America being a colony of Japan?

There also could be many side benefits to the American people taking this decisive action of balancing our foreign trade. Our government then would be in a stronger position to negotiate some fair and just trade deals. That is, if the negotiators didn't have their eye on a future job as a Japanese lobbyist.

I would not want to imply that all of our trading partners are unfair. Many countries are most fair. Recently, we have seen the good cooperation of Taiwan to buy more and more American products to try to balance our trade.

We do not seem to see the same attitude in actions by Japan, Germany or Korea. We do get a lot of kind words, but little real action in this regard.

Many so called experts will say none of these actions I have suggested will ever happen. Many of these same people thought Eastern Europe was forever tied to Communism and the U.S.S.R.

But it was "We the People" in Eastern Europe who made the great change. We can do the same in America when we have suffered enough or use our common sense and do it now.

I can just hear the "freetraders" saying this solution is terrible. They will suggest it is taking us back to the dark ages. But you should realize that this is just the strategy our major trade advisory—Japan—has practiced for years. The Japanese buy mostly Japanese goods, not imported goods.

I was shocked to hear some time ago that Japan's total imports of **manufactured goods** was less than Switzerland's. When you realize there are over 120 million people in Japan and only about **seven** million in Switzerland, you appreciate how effective Japan's protectionist policy is.

We are all aware of the potential problems as we switch more and more of our purchases to American manufactured goods. But as you stop and think about it, we often take steps in our buying habits to send messages and we haven't suffered much.

Many Americans changed their buying habits by not investing in or refusing to purchase goods made by companies that had strong ties to the South African system of Apartheid, that are known violators of environmental laws, or pay sub-minimum wages for illegal immigrant workers. Americans even change their buying habits when confronted with companies that advertise on television shows they find distasteful. We even went without Iranian and Russian caviar.

We hear the comment that if we don't buy a Japanese product we will have to go without many items. Fortunately, that isn't true. At a recent meeting where we discussed that subject the **only** item most people would have to do without was a video camera. VCRs, Televisions, HiFi equipment, and so forth are made in many countries. Even countries which open their markets to American manufactured goods.

I'm sure that if we declare the manufacture of video cameras an "infant industry" in America under GATT Article XVIII and put a large duty on imported video cameras, we can probably get some company to start manufacturing the product in America.

But by far the easiest and quickest way to switch manufacturing jobs to America is to buy only American made cars. That is cars with over 75% American content. And there are many fine American cars. Even **one** of the Honda cars may qualify as an American car.

Just think, in January 1991, our total trade deficit was the same as the value of imported cars! I realize a few would find it hard to swallow if they bought only American cars, but so be it. This will really get the instant attention of Japan. But they will have no one to **criticize except** maybe the **American consumer** who has been their **life saver** for the past 20 years. Suddenly, they will have no surplus funds to buy up American companies and real estate. We won't need their funds to buy treasury bills as we will no longer have a trade deficit. We will collect more taxes as we will have more Americans working for American manufacturers who all will pay more taxes.

The American consumers have no idea of the great power they have. I think this power is even greater here in 1991 following the Gulf War. We saw a new pride in America. We saw the greatest outpouring of patriotism in many years. We were proud of our country once again. We learned once again how great our people are.

Now let's turn that surge of nationalism into solving the problems in our country. These problems will not be solved by government give-away programs. They will only be solved if we can give our people good jobs. Manufacturing jobs that add value to a product. Not service jobs. When this is done, many of our problems facing us today will gradually fade away. We cannot expect our government to solve the problems but it could help. We can't expect our businesses and manufacturers to do it all. They need the help of "We the People." The only quick as well as longer range solution is to:

- **Declare a buying holiday on imported goods.**

Not all imported goods, only those from countries where they have barriers against our products and companies. Or they have a **major** trade surplus with America. We don't want to hurt them, we just want them to play fair. Even though this book is mainly about Japan, many of the above points apply to some other countries but to a much lesser degree.

What I suggest can be a grass-roots movement that builds on a little U.S. nationalism like the display after the Gulf War, not unlike the nationalism that the Japanese have about buying Japanese goods. Remember how Americans handled the Arab oil crisis in the 70's? The change in energy use habits and the amount of energy conservation work people did on their homes and businesses was phenomenal. It slowed the uptrend of energy use for a number of years until the economy boomed again and cheap energy made us lazy again. American actions caused the former Saudi Oil Minister Sheik Yamani to change his rhetoric from saying that Americans were energy wasters to saying that Americans should buy more oil from the OPEC countries. Today, we hear similar talk from Japan that our balance-of-trade problems are all of our own making. To be sure our own economic policies skew consumer actions toward buying low-cost imports and buying rather than saving. **Quietly, reducing the purchase of Japanese goods is the only easy effective way to start to solve our problems quickly.** We don't need any government action or approval. We don't need the approval or consent of the media. We don't need the agreement of the Japanese. Just Do It—"We the People."

I am confident that if enough of us are really concerned for our fellow Americans, we can make this work. Every time two Japanese cars are imported to America, about one American manufacturing job is lost. It's not just the American auto worker but all the other suppliers and support people who suffer. Similarly, manufacturing jobs are lost due to other imports.

We can be sure that if "We the People" actively pursue the plan of **not** buying Japanese products for a few months, we will begin to see the Japanese dealing with America in a more fair manner. The Japanese are very smart people and they know how they would suffer if American consumers "Just Say No" to Japanese products.

I am not suggesting that you stop buying imported Japanese goods because you **don't like** the Japanese. However, you may not want to buy their goods because you don't like what the Japanese **do.** Or you don't buy Japanese goods because they honor the Arab boycott of dealing with Israel, which is illegal in America, or because their leaders say most minorities in America are not very intelligent, or because the Japanese companies supported Apartheid South Africa when American and European companies pulled out. Some of those reasons for not buying their products are very proper and correct if the Japanese have offended you or your principles, or if they have refused to permit your products to be freely sold in Japan such as rice, citrus fruits, beef, cigarettes, automobiles, etc.

But the **real basic reason** you should stop buying Japanese goods is that you want to have a **good job** for yourself, for your wife or husband, for your son or daughter, for your mother or father or your neighbor, or for those 500,000 United Auto Workers who have lost their jobs in the last few years, or the other estimated million or so workers in other support industries that lost their manufacturing jobs.

It isn't a matter of **prejudice,** it's a matter of **survival.** Don't wait for our government to help. Don't look for business to help, except to make better products. You need to do it yourself. Just decide you are going to buy products that make good jobs in America so you can eat and survive.

Some people say one product is slightly better than another but—does it really matter? Some people say one beer is better than another but can you really tell the difference? And, even if you can, how important is it to you compared to what kind of job you have? The same applies to almost all products and your life and future.

One way to start this program to support the American worker would be for everyone who stopped buying Japanese products to put a 'Blue Ribbon' around the tree in their front yard or on their apartment door or on their American car.

'Blue Ribbons' have always been given to winners so it is quite symbolic.

The Japanese won't be able to complain to our government or to our businesses for this action as they will not be involved (except maybe for some quiet support). The Japanese can only complain to the American consumer who made them so successful. Then we might buy even less.

After a few years, we should be able to relax this program as trade matters even out. Hopefully, then we can develop good fair relations between our countries and the people. By then, America will no longer be **Japan's New Colony.** ◻

Epilogue:
WE THE PEOPLE

SHORTLY AFTER I finished writing this book, I couldn't help but be made aware of dramatic new events that demonstrated the great power of **"We the People."**

As was noted in earlier chapters, we saw the power of **"We the People"** that brought about the freedom of Eastern Europe in 1989 and 1990. However, the most earth shaking exhibition of the power of **"We the People"** came in August 1991, when the people in the USSR showed they had powers far greater than the Communist party or the leaders of the USSR government or military. The collapse and failure of 70 years of Communist rule illustrated what **"We the People"** can bring about. **We really do have a new world order.**

This gives me great hope that the suggestions I outlined in Chapter 16 can come to reality in America with the freedom and power of **"We the People."** ☐